T0369948

SEXISTENCE

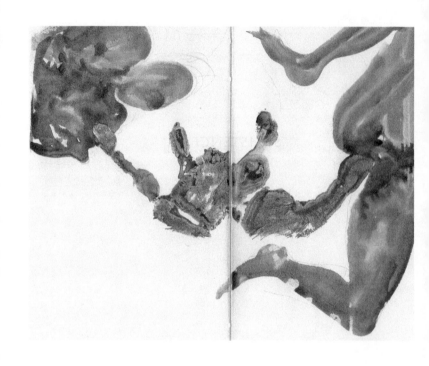

Sexistence

Jean-Luc Nancy
TRANSLATED BY STEVEN MILLER

FORDHAM UNIVERSITY PRESS   NEW YORK 2021

This book was originally published in French as Jean-Luc Nancy, *Sexistence*, Copyright © Éditions Galilée, 2017.

Frontispiece © Miquel Barceló, 2017

Fordham University Press has no responsibility for the persistence or accuracy of URLs for external or third-party Internet websites referred to in this publication and does not guarantee that any content on such websites is, or will remain, accurate or appropriate.

Fordham University Press also publishes its books in a variety of electronic formats. Some content that appears in print may not be available in electronic books.

Visit us online at www.fordhampress.com.

Library of Congress Control Number: 2021904182

Printed in the United States of America

23 22 21   5 4 3 2 1

First edition

(For their reading and their advice, I thank Cécile Bourguignon, Rosaria Caldarone, Ariane Chottin, Zeynep Direk, Mathilde Girard, Juan-Manuel Garrido, and Hélène Nancy)

Contents

SEXISTENCE

Preliminaries

nothing so much as this the more we enjoy it
the more concupiscence becomes our fate[1]

A

Fatality?

Every genre of sex has its preliminaries: one approaches, one considers, one scents, one lets oneself be approached, brushed, and stroked in the various senses of that word. There is a word in Classical Latin, *blandiri*, that the Latinate languages long retained, in which the caress mixes with speech, each changing place with the other and sinuously looking to merge in the silence of a kiss. Montaigne speaks of "the seductive blandishments of immoderate pleasure."[2]

It happens that things progress and then without notice or precaution one goes right for the goal, albeit not without this transgression itself constituting a defiant approach, a superb manner of declaring that one can and will pass on the preliminaries. One thereby designates the threshold even more clearly. Because *liminaries* pertain to the threshold,

1

they happen on the threshold, and what precedes them must arrange and ready access to the threshold. Blandishments and kisses not only open access, they already engage it, experience it, and anticipate it.

The preliminaries, too, are already part of what they precede, prepare, hold up, and overtake at the same time. This is the case, at least, with sexual preliminaries; but we should also examine whether it holds true for all preliminaries, and whether it is always the modulation of a characteristic that most properly emerges in sex: an anticipation that does not merely project but precedes or assumes the precocious character of a premature enjoyment with regard to a fulfilled coitus.

But what precisely is the fulfillment in question? The possibility of fertilization? A sharing of enjoyment? In what order of finality, destination, disorientation, or confusion do we find ourselves?

In truth, we have arrived at the crux of what is called "sex": neither sexual difference, nor different sexualities, but sex itself—sex as an act and not an organ or function. To the extent that it happens—no matter how, as relation or as anticipation, as enjoyment or as disappointment. To the extent that it demands to happen, that it demands to be "had" not as a need must be satisfied but as a pressure exerts itself, as an excitation excites itself [*s'excite*], exalts itself [*s'exalte*], exasperates itself [*s'exaspère*], and in sum—perhaps to say nothing further—exists itself [*s'existe*]: it arises and propels itself into existence, which is, at least, one of its most energetic mainsprings—albeit, as well, the least necessary, or the most excessive [*excédent*] (if not actually maddening [*excédant*]).

The organ thus welcomes the difference of the stranger into my body: it is always the organ of my ruin, and this truth is so original that neither the heart, the cen-

*tral organ of life, nor the sex, the first organ of life, can
escape it . . . A true man has no sex for he must be his
sex. As soon as the sex becomes an organ, it becomes
foreign to me, abandons me, acquiring thereby the
arrogant autonomy of a swollen object full of itself.
This swelling of the sex become a separate object is a
kind of castration . . . The organ: place of loss because
its center always has the form of an orifice. The organ
always functions as an embouchure.*[3]

The crux is indeed this: that sex is an exigency and an excess; that its demand—never quenched because it was never
destined to be—is announced in the difficulty of the word
dira as Lucretius employs it: a term of augury, designating
a deathly presage but also the power of a furor. A furor itself
both bright and dark, an augury of both favor and fright because—as Lucretius develops—what appeases it unleashes
it anew and it always finds itself on its own threshold. Such
is its fatality:

*Craving for water or for bread is easily satisfied.
But of a human face's bloom and beauty, what
        comes in
For the body to enjoy? Just images, flimsy and thin,
And the wind often snatches even this scrap of hope
        away.
As in a dream, when a man drinks, trying to allay
His thirst, but gets no real liquid to douse his body's
        fire,
And struggles pointlessly after mere images of water,
And though he gulps and gulps from a gushing
        stream, his throat is dry,
So Venus teases with images—lovers can't satisfy
The flesh however they devour each other with the eye,
Nor with hungry hands roving the body can they reap*

> *Anything from the supple limbs that they can take*
>   *and keep.*
> *Lastly, when their limbs are tangled, and they*
>   *pluck youth's bloom,*
> *And bodies have a foretaste of the pleasures that*
>   *now loom,*
> *And Venus is about to sow the woman's field with seed,*
> *They grasp each other and mix the moisture of their*
>   *mouths in greed,*
> *And panting heavily, press teeth in lips, but all in*
>   *vain—*
> *There's nothing of the other they can rub off and*
>   *retain.*
> *Nor can one body wholly enter the other and pass*
>   *away—*[4]

What Bataille will designate much later as erotic comedy is already staged here, staged as the drama that, in reality, this comedy designates for Bataille himself—the drama or perhaps, we'll try to return this, tragedy in the most powerful sense of the term: that of sense fulfilling itself in the passage to the limit of sense itself, in accord with its ownmost fatality.

This passage, when it is not the passing away of death, is that of sex—or that of language. For, the latter exposes what sex without language is content to impose: an interminable pursuit, running that chases its own course.[5]

This course, ever again, thrusts and urges itself forth because it has no end: it does not pass anywhere but proves and approves itself in its very passage. Lucretius clearly discerns what happens: he pursues, with a prosodic haste or rush that seems itself to lose breath before or in what it says:

> *For it seems sometimes that this is what they*
>   *struggle to essay,*

Such do they clasp in the chains of Venus, greedily
    and tight,
While limbs go limp, melted with the heat of their
    delight.[6]

"For it seems": *videntur*, the lovers appear and thus will always appear to seek a union that they fail to achieve; and yet the inexhaustible return of erotic furor ends up showing that they also—or even, instead—seek the renewal of their own avidity and the turbulence they share—which Lucretius will later call *communia gaudia*, shared joys.[7]

One might risk saying: not communion but rather *comme-union* ["as"-union or "like"-union, perhaps even *akinship*—Trans.]. They appear to want union but they want its simulacrum—if not its simulation—whereby springs the ardor that lends élan to the so acute pleasure of desire. Also:

At last, when loins erupt forth from the gathering
    desire,
They are allowed a brief reprieve from passion's
    raging fire.
But then the fever starts again, madness must soon
    return,
When yet again they seek to have the thing for
    which they yearn.
They can discover no device to conquer their disease—[8]

B

Liberation?

There is a fatality of sex, which first appears to form an impasse or a block: it does not lead to a durable goal and never stops claiming its due, only ever obtained for an instant at best. But the sense of fatality goes beyond condemnation: it signifies what is said, pronounced and announced, what sets a tone. Tone, here, is that of a tension that doesn't even know what it tends toward, what it wants to attain or touch—*contingere*: with what it wishes to meet up, against what it wishes to brush, to the contingency of what contact it aspires.

Sex, in other words, ignores what is properly at stake in touch: it is made of touch, through and through, and touch is all it does (tact, proximity, intimacy, dexterity, grazing, caress, thrill, tremor, trouble) but all it knows about touch is élan, thrust, itch, hunger, and appetite. It knows nothing else, neither where it comes from nor where it's going. Nothing except that it is agitated, animated, and excited. It troubles and in troubling troubles itself: it diverts and diverges—even the most obvious goal, that of having children, is not so clearly linked to the violence of its appeal. If this appeal had to be understood as the ruse of biological reason, it would be hard to understand, on the one hand, why sex knows so little about itself and, on the other hand, its skill at turning, whenever it wants, away from procreation.

The less sex knows itself the more its experience is powerful and insistent. This is also why it requires preliminaries to pass to the unknown, to surrender to its fatality and its contingency: making love is no more grounded than declaring love. When declaring love, one knows nothing but being carried away and opening a perspective without end; and the same goes for making love, except that it's possible to imagine an end to it—even though no one knows what will bring it to an end, where it will end, or whether it will truly be an end. In addition, making love can always engage one to declare it, while declaring it engages one in principle to make it.

Fatality reveals itself to be ambiguous: love promises

everything—along with sex; sex promises an end while hiding that it might become infinite. Every promise is liable not to be kept: this is its nature. But, here, each promise hangs on the exorbitant dimension that it conceals: a fulfillment in excess of any achievement, completeness or completion. Whence it becomes a kind of promise of promise: someone in love promises that they will promise without end, the lover promises a pleasure without measure.

Love and sex are almost the same thing and yet are separate, or at least divided, because sex can offer itself as limited in scope—in duration, in context, or in type of relation—which love excludes in principle. In different cultures, this division assumes very diverse forms and styles. Nonetheless, it would seem that this unstable division nearly always comes into play, even when what Western culture promotes as "love" has been largely diverted into bonds of conjugal or familial belonging. The force of desire—of this desire that polarizes all the possible values of the word "desire"—manifests itself with or without any affective, spiritual, or social form. It is even the first thing that comes to mind upon the mere utterance of the word "sex," offered in its nudity: a violence of covetousness, avidity, rutting, raging appetite, a vehemence or exigency linked to the representation of luxury, lasciviousness, even vice or bestiality (along with the grins, the laughter, or the snickering of people who disavow such things).

*

I will be told that this is no longer where we are; that sexual liberation has delivered us from such images of excess, measurelessness, obsession and frenzy linked to dramatic, perilous, or unwholesome pursuits. Sex is now the name for a set of practices recognized as both secret and exposed, which we are supposed to care for, help flourish, and keep vital. Emancipated from civil or religious constraints, arising only from personal disposition and choice, sexualities would be analogous to athletic, touristic, or aesthetic activities and preferences. At the same time, these registers keep intersecting in a sort of voluptuous multimedia mash-up of virtual reality orgasms, sex toys brought on vacation to some palm beach, and psychology tests that reveal what type of lover you are, how best to excite your partner or how to make your relationship last.

It is quite clear that this glossy erethism and worldwide priapism constitute the eloquent symptoms of slavery rather than liberation. One can and must rejoice that the forms of prohibition, repression, discrimination, and culpability, which shackled the morals of another age, have been lifted. Nevertheless, this emancipation, like others, does not really know from what or toward what it is liberated. Whence the febrility with which this liberation goes around promoting a sex that it ceaselessly shows to be fragile, delicate, complex, and fleeting.

A critique almost as widespread and almost as "commodified" as pornography itself denounces our society of consumerist enjoyment and sexual consumption. It reduces the word and the idea of "enjoyment" to nothing more than the poverty of a devouring fervor, the unhappy search for an insatiable satisfaction. Enjoyment bespeaks the ravages of an ego reduced to its own repletion; and the transformation of capitalism into speculative bulimia and financial engorgement—through the choking of the consumerist model itself—forms the background of a civilization devoted to stuffing itself like a goose to end up suffocated, like the goose, in its own fat.

Indeed, aside from financial speculation and energetic frenzy, there are two notable regimes of overconsumption:

that of sex and that of art. Which is to say, two regimes each placed under the sign of what might be called an exponential nomination: saying "sex" or saying "art" I refer less to something than to a beyond of all things. I name a sort of thing-in-itself or a Parousia, an absolute presence, a pleroma or plethora—plenitude, fullness, infinite reiteration, principle of unlimited pleasure. Pleasure is revealed in its plenitude of desire: it is less what charms and seduces than what flares up in pursuit, in ceaseless intensification.

Art is liberated from its own forms ("beauty" only matters when violated) while sex is liberated from its shame, secrets, and mystery. The economy, for its part, is liberated from what Marx called the fetishism of the commodity because the fetish (exchange value) is very clearly identified with use value, or absorbs it, and vice versa. It produces a general denudation, and even an initially obscene denudation, deprived of the modesty that is the form of sexual force.

The human race is drunk on its sexuality: something that is, at this point, and always more so, surprising. The desire to be . . . what it is, i.e. sexuated: screaming from the rooftops and plastering the walls with their sexual character, representing their sexual difference as if they didn't yet really "know that they are naked."[9]

*

We would thus be liberated, on the one hand, from something that weighed down, repressed, masked, and deceived—but also, on the other hand, from something that posited, inserted into an order, and gave meaning (albeit mysterious or disturbing). This double deliverance is complex and even obscure in its entanglement. Neither side can unburden itself from the other. One can neither be content to "enjoy

without shackles," as they said in May '68—which, inciden-
tally, was in no way a consumerist slogan but a pro-vocation
to thinking—nor to suppose that the denudation in question
would be an elementary reality entrusted to the discretion
of a techno-economic machine that some believe can be
encapsulated in the notion of "biopower."

This is all too elementary, precisely. Or rather, the elementary is always an abstraction. Much like nudity, considered as pure stripping bare, is an abstraction. All denudation
is the index of an even more intimate denudation, perhaps
bottomless or unattainable. Which also means that the various ways of reacting to "sexual liberation," whether they
claim to be ethical, political, or aesthetic, are precisely no
more than "reactions."

C

Philosophy?

This is the point at which the preliminaries begin to become
liminaries—that is, to pass to the threshold, at least to tarry
on it or in it, within its aperture. We cannot help but feel
that something other is at stake than what remains poorly
said so long as it is said in terms of liberation or deliverance
or disengagement from liberation itself.

To all appearances, there are two statements that must
now be made: the first is that the uninhibited and as it were
naturalist consideration of sex does not date from the consumerist and globalized turn of the liberal and technical political economy. It came from long before: at least two centu-
ries before.[10] The second statement, on the contrary, recalls
that sex played a major and exemplary philosophical role at

very beginnings of philosophy but was soon abandoned and then nearly forgotten or limited to almost nothing.

Let us take up and begin to unpack these two statements that are impossible not to recognize.

1.

The first statement exposes to us the soft curve of a movement, an élan, and an insistence that goes at least from Sade and Fourier to Freud by way of Krafft-Ebing and the *Anthropophyteia*.[11] For his contemporaries, Freud was less the inventor of the "unconscious" than of sex—the "inventor" in the sense that this word designates he who finds an abandoned object, a brick, a treasure.

> [Mrs. Apley questions her husband about a book that their daughter had been reading, written by a certain Dr. Freud.]
> —*What's it about?*
> —*Well, it's about the mind and the human relationships that affect the mind.*
> —*What sort of relationships?*
> —*I hardly know how to put it . . . I shall have to resort to a word that I've never used in your presence. It seems to be very largely a book about—sex.*
> [Mrs. Apley makes a little noise in her throat before saying:]
> —*Oh! But how can he write a whole book about—* that?[12]

What was this abandoned object, then? Indeed, it was less sexuality than the energy that subtends and traverses it. The Freudian enterprise is, in an essential manner, an energetics. What is determined as the drive, in at least two different forms (pleasure and destruction), derives its force from a "displaceable energy, which, neutral in itself, can be added to a qualitatively differentiated erotic or destructive impulse, and augment its total cathexis." To this, Freud immediately adds: "Without assuming the existence of a displaceable energy of this kind we can make no headway."[13]

And later, he specifies that it can be supposed this energy proceeds from a "narcissistic store of libido," that is, "desexualized Eros."[14] This singular Eros is only "desexualized" to the extent that it hasn't yet turned toward an outside. It is thus equally "presexual." Nonetheless, it is "Eros" and this "Eros" constitutes the preexisting reserve, the store, or the resource of a differentiated libidinal existence directed toward other beings (or "objects") than the "ego" bound to the mass of the "id." (Freud specifies that this energy is "no doubt active in both the ego and the id."[15]) Here we find ourselves at the origin or the principle, at the most ancient archaeology of what we gladly call "a subject," or of what Heidegger calls *Dasein*: the existent who opens its own "there," its world and its way of being in it.

Freud will go on to say that the drives are his myths, in that they are based on hypotheses or fictions that no thinking of the origin can avoid. I will return to this point. For the moment, let us merely consider this: Freud *invents*, he finds a neglected origin. God—to name his name—the very ancient "prime mover" who grew into the "creator" and the "source of life," this God who, as Nietzsche understood, our metaphysics and our science have killed, gives way to an energy that is unassignable and indeterminate but that pushes and pulses, that impels the world and us in it, unto itself.[16]

2.

This brings us to the second statement: what Freud calls "metapsychology" along the lines of "metaphysics" opens a new register that, beyond the psyche, concerns being and existence.

Many were the philosophers, until the 1950s, who saw no more in psychoanalysis than a reduction of anthropology to sexuality. They did not see that this reduction was in fact an extension, an amplification of philosophical (or metaphysical) exploration and desire. There where a Supreme Being had seemed to furnish an origin—and only seemed, for it created as many real difficulties as apparent answers—the *archaic* had to be envisaged with the rigor required by something that lies as far back as one can go. Freud's Eros is not a god but rather a demon; it defies us to measure ourselves with an energy impossible to capture and to assign—a force as impetuously free (and thus not "liberatable") as it is imperiously attractive (as "fatal" as an irresistible appeal).

> *. . . with the heroic hesitations of a traveler embarking on an exploration or of a desperate man killing himself, with a feeling of faintness, I would clear an unknown and I thought fatal path within myself, until the moment when a natural trail like that left by a snail added itself to the leaves of the wild black currant that leaned in toward me.*[17]

Accordingly, Plato's Socrates, instructed by Diotima,[18] attributed to Eros the most singular among all powers, that of arousing desire and lending it an impulsion that can raise up to the most ideal beauties. Freud never ceased to extol this Eros. He even suggested that the archaeology of Platonic Eros might lead back to the Hindu idea of a "Self" who, sad to be alone, divides itself into two sexes in order to gain joy.[19]

From Plato to Freud, or from the *Upanishads* to us, we discover the stakes of what is called "sex" in a sense that precedes and exceeds the sexual function. In a remarkably strange manner, philosophy finds itself implicated therein:

having lent Eros a westward course, it seems immediately to leave it behind and then, much later, to regain it in a "joy" that Lacan would call "jouissance," although neither philosophy itself nor the metamorphosis of philosophy called metapsychology have penetrated its secret, doing no more than confirm its nature as a secret. Not so much in the sense of something hidden, kept in the shadows, but rather in the sense of what enlightens as the very origin of light.

*

How to understand philosophy's abandonment of Eros?[20] I will make do with a single indication: in the *Phaedrus*, Plato describes sexual transport and its stakes in a manner that will not recur in philosophy. Just a short citation from the dialogue:

> And after the lover has spent some time doing this, staying near the boy . . . then the spring that feeds the stream Zeus named "Desire" when he was in love with Ganymede begins to flow mightily in the lover and its partly absorbed by him, and when he is filled it overflows and runs away outside him . . . that is how the stream of beauty goes back to the beautiful boy and sets him aflutter. It enters through his eyes, which are its natural route to the soul; there it waters the passages for the wings, starts the wings growing, and fills the soul of the loved one with love in return.[21]

A little earlier, the same text specifies that beauty is the sole superior reality that manifests itself in the sensible, where it triggers the keenest appetites as well as the highest aspirations. But if *phronesis*—that is, judgment, discernment, wisdom—"came through our sight as clearly as

beauty does," it would awaken a "terribly powerful love."[22]
Everything will have proceeded, after Plato, as if philosophical erotics were entirely turned toward the insensible—all
frenzy toward *phronesis* (which is not a play on words but an
etymological derivation!).

In Plato himself, the erotic is beset with a very serious conflict between immediate appetite and the desire for beauty.
This conflict can itself be analyzed—psychoanalyzed—as a
tension between Socrates's femininity and Plato's masculin-
ity.[23] The thinking of the Idea is divided between sensible
Form, itself sensual, and the Concept . . .

At a certain moment, philosophical frenzy itself destroyed the supposition of a supersensible truth. It recognized it as an effect of language and recognized language
itself as bounded by existence that cannot be reduced to a
single signification. "Being" is not a real attribute, but only,
at most, logical: Kant's affirmation[24] opens an era in which
Reason must itself be considered as *Trieb*, drive, urge, tension, and desire toward an "unconditional" that ultimately
shows itself to consist in nothing other than its own impulsion. Called "will" by Schopenhauer and then by Nietzsche,
it will re-emerge as "drive"—not without going by way of
"labor power" in Marx and the "leap" in Kierkegaard. Certainly, as well, it goes by way of the "parallel differences"
of Deleuze and of Derrida—differentiation and différance
that at least have in common that they uphold a tension, an
impulsion, or a pulsation.[25]

In this sense, Freud appears as a double inflection point
in the history of thought: on the one hand, "psychoanalysis" opens a site for archaeological and clinical work within
a space that hitherto had been represented as that of logic
without *archè* and of "sound mind"; and on the other hand,
metaphysics metamorphoses into "metapsychology"—a
chain of "metas" that augurs a movement beyond thought

(whether or not it's called philosophy) into which we are just beginning to penetrate.

Between the two edges or two aspects of this dehiscence a perhaps incommensurable relation (like the sexual relation for Lacan) is played out. I remain exclusively on the side of philosophy in which I am engaged not only by my profession but also by the meta-chain that I just evoked. No doubt the future will transform yet again this entire transformation in which we are caught up.

Freud himself says a few things about this dehiscence. In a footnote to "Dynamics of Transference," he indicates that "*daimon* and *tuchè*[26] (a Greek formula that he writes in the original and that signifies "demon and chance") governs all human existence. Psychoanalysis, he specifies, has more to say about *tuchè*[27] than about *daimon*, on the subject of which it's hardly possible to do more than repeat what is already known. This declaration is immediately displaced by remarks on the interdependence of the two instances. Nonetheless, *daimon*, what is proper to a singular existence (of a supposed "subject"), is here considered as already known, which can only mean: known as unknowable, as the singularity of a demi-divinity or of a genius who gives a unique impulsion to an existence.

We can say that philosophy (whether done by an author known as a psychoanalyst or a philosopher) is concerned with the *daimon* and thus with what has always already been known—for example, the demonicity or the demoniacality of Eros—, and what, precisely because it's always known—for example, by Diotima—remains always to be said anew.

Now we are approaching the end of these preliminaries: as one can see, already it's Diotima who will have prepared—against her will or without her consent—a return to what, in sex, will henceforward be less "liberated" than exposed to a renewed thought [*pensée*]—or thrust [*poussée*].

D

Drive?

The approach to the threshold—I dare not say the "attainment" of it—would thus be signaled by the word "drive" [*pulsion*]. A whole semantic family surrounds it—pulsation, impulsion, expulsion, compulsion, pulsar, pulse, push, shoot or thrust [*poussée*].[28]

This a redoubtable word, much like its equivalents in other languages. It designates at once a force and its effect; its notion is situated between a source of energy and the energy itself, added to which is a value of élan, dispatch, excitation. If the drive consists of energy, then it's primarily in the Greek sense of *en-ergeia*, a putting to work and into action that remains not entirely actualized or conclusive, always retaining the *dynamis*, a "power" itself not limited to "potential" but effective in its exercise. Added as well, as the semantic family demonstrates, is a rhythmic value linked to an emphasis upon the impetus of the pulse, the rap or the beat of a given élan.

> *My lover at my side whose oil tames my hands, my*
> *   soul,*
> *My strength rises in surrender, my honor in*
> *   submission,*
> *My skill in the instinct of your rhythm.*
> *The lead dancer centers the force at the prow of his*
> *   sex,*
> *Like the bold hunter of sea cows.*
> *Beat the rhythm of bells, beat tongues, beat oars*
> *Dance of the Master Oarsman.*
> *Ah! His pirogue is worthy of Fadyoutt's triumphal*
> *   choruses.*[29]

The drive drives and it is itself driven. Or rather, it is itself the driving force, the impulse. In the aftermath of Kant, from Fichte to Nietzsche and Husserl, we could follow the way in which the drive of reason becomes the act of the subject, of nature and/or of spirit.

This is not the place to undertake a study of this history—at bottom, that of the *daimon* in Freud and Plato—that is, ultimately, and to say it once again in other terms, the history of the destination of man, and even of life, in the absence of God as well as the gods. Destination: not destiny along the lines of a petrified notion of predestination but rather the *fatum* that I have evoked, the speech that announces and sets the tone of a send-off, an address that is relayed to existence without thereby determining the latter as a process with rules set in advance. Even the gods, in any event, and even God are never limited to predestination: they have always left something undecided, the possibility of adverse chance, a diversion or a conversion. In destiny there is always what Derrida calls a *destinerrance*. This is how we should understand the interaction of the *daimon* and the *tuchè*.

Accordingly, what can be found throughout the history of the *destinerrant* thrust would derive in large measure from the indetermination of the drive. An indetermination that primarily manifests itself as the inadequation of the drive to itself. It pushes, and thus its force must be oriented, and yet it does not push toward any goal. Nietzsche says that "every drive is unintelligent, such that it has no use for a perspective . . . the drives don't think about what's advantageous for the whole ego; they act against our advantage, against the ego—and often for the ego—innocent in either case!"[30]

Not only does the drive exert itself or can it exert itself without direction, but by virtue of the fact that it pulses it also necessarily repulses something, another force or other forces that resist it. If its initial élan seems perforce (in spite of what Nietzsche claims) to correspond to an interest or an expectation on the part of the thing (or he or she) that it pushes, it is also entirely possible and even probable that resistances will cause it difficulty and make it suffer. The drive requires a tension; and tension, in principle, is opposed to satisfaction: this is precisely the question that Freud examines with regard to "forepleasure" in sexual desire and "gain in pleasure" in the drive's use of aesthetic form. There can be, then, inherent to the force of the drive, a particular form that takes pleasure in the very unpleasure that it generates. As we know, the duality of Eros and Thanatos does not prevent Freud from considering their interactions or their mixtures (*Triebmischung*).[31]

It might be said that the drive suffers twice over: from the resistance that it encounters or provokes, from its own tension, and ultimately from the constant tearing at itself in which it consists (or rather, in which it insists). In this sense, Thanatos does not merely counter Eros: it is integral to it.

To the traits that I ascribe to self-inadequation, another must be added: it can be better elaborated on the basis of a notion that doesn't often bring the drive into play but rather might be considered as its effect: Heidegger's "being-thrown."[32] Ek-sistence, as he suggests we write the word, consists in an ejection, an expulsion, or an exile.[33] The ek-sistent is not thrown outside a place nor thrown by a foreign will: its being consists entirely in this being-thrown. Outside nothing and by nothing or no one. Undoubtedly, it comes from a womb or an act of copulation (already sex); but copulation itself was ex-pressed in the womb or as this womb that, in turn, lets be ex-tracted a new ex-perience of being. Which is a manner of saying that there is a primordial drive; and yet, such a drive does not preexist existence but rather forces and forms its throw, its expulsion unto being.

What Heidegger goes on to formulate as "anxiety" and as

"care," which do not cease to be thrown—sent, addressed, expedited toward its most proper absence of goal, toward its exposure to everything and nothing—to the impossible as to its ownmost possibility—they also do not cease to have a libidinal, propulsive, or pulsating nature. Which also means "thrust" (*poussée*)—both as the name for an act and as the epithet for an object or person subjected to such an act. The drive pertains as much to reception as to action.

A pulsar (pulsating star[34]) is a celestial body that periodically shines very brightly. It is plausible to say that every existence is such a celestial body, plausible also to wonder to what degree all the realities in the world participate in such a pulsation. This is to say, in fact, to what degree every reality (living or not) is fundamentally constituted of an ex-pulsion of nothing toward nothing—of *res* toward *res* that is nothing other than being in general, that is to say, in particular. As Schelling writes: "The principle of life did come from outside into organic matter (as if by infusion)—(an inapt and yet widespread conception)—but rather, inversely, this principle molded and made organic matter its own. Likewise, while life is individualized as singular beings and, in turn, gives them individuality, it becomes a principle that can no longer be explained on the basis of the organization itself and whose agency is only revealed to the individual sensibility as an always bustling drive."[35]

In other words, the drive is nothing other than existence itself—eksisting, existing—in its character as upsurge or multiplication, as an origin that can't be allocated outside of its own opening and its thrust. Among all the historical figures and facets of the divine, it would most resemble that of the first, uncreated monad, all of whose incessant radiation produces the created monads.

Drive, divine radiation, thrust open to the infinity of its renewal and to the abyss of its destination, fatal in every sense—this is how the drive is proposed or exposed, thereby inseparable from sex. Led by the adventures of modern thought since Plato, we thus arrive at a sort of ontology of sex—or at the consideration of a *sexistence*.

> *Her name was Nadja Yurenieva and she was nineteen. That very night she made love with Ansky, once Ivanov had managed to fall asleep after several glasses of vodka. They did it in Ansky's room and anyone who saw them would have said that they fucked as if they had only a few hours left to live. Actually, Nadja Yure- nieva fucked like many Muscovites that year of 1936 and Boris Ansky fucked as if when all hope was lost he had suddenly found his only true love. Neither of the two thought (or wanted to think) about death, but both moved, twined their limbs, communed, as if they were on the edge of the abyss.*[36]

E

Unsayable?

Sex tends toward its own exasperation, exacerbated desire, as an obsessive return or else as the refusal of its own furor, anx- iety, and spasm. The power of acceptance that it supposes is as great as that of its impulsion. It knows that in enjoying it might fizzle as well as flare up. It can become too difficult or exigent for itself. It is, at every moment, on the edge of an impossibility as its most proper possibility.

But we must not omit to specify that it is addressed to the other and also is received from the other. Even if it seems to occur alone. The other—no matter their gender—is al- ready contained in the drive: a stranger to itself as well as to consciousness and to the will, even when it seems to exert itself with complete mastery (at a certain extreme of mastery, it gets lost).

Sex is addressed to the other and is received from the other at the most intimate recess of oneself. This means above all that in the other person something other than the person is in question. The question is rather of the exorbitant nature of the thrust itself, which can only push and pulse infinitely—whether this infinity is that of reproduction or that of jouissance (which are perhaps the same thing, as we shall see).

In all rigor, it is out of reach. One doesn't arrive. One arrives by not arriving. One is at the edge, before or after. It's like the coming of the Messiah whom one cannot recognize. It's like what one cannot say because it doesn't pertain to saying.

Lacan makes lovers say: "'I ask you to refuse what I offer you because that's not it' . . . 'That's not it' is the very cry by which the jouissance obtained is distinguished from the jouissance expected."[37] We might add: that's not the *id*, in fact, from which the drive arises and to which it returns, because, in the id there is no one anymore or no one yet. But lovers, when they cry out, already know this.

They know it just as we know that speech always says, at its edge, that beyond speech, accessible only to it, there is a cry that crashes into silence. This is why language and sex are intimately linked: they have the same destination or the same *destinerrance*. A cry or a song emerges from the body, an exclamation on the threshold of ecstasy and expiration. It occurs as failure *and* as success. Such is the double *fatum* of sex, the best example of which is existence.

How is existence exemplary of sex? Because sex is continuous with life, with the animal, with the vegetable, and— why not—with the pulsar? And its twin, speech, sets itself apart and jumps into the midst of it all.

Sometimes a poem knows how to say something of the cry:

My husband approached the bed,
My sari's knot untied itself,
My sari, held by slackened girdle,
Somehow just rested on my hips.
I know that much now, friend!
But once again locked in his embrace,
"Who is he?" "Who am I?" "Is this lovemaking?"
Of this I have not the slightest recollection.[38]

Our preliminaries thus conclude. Let us begin, or begin again. For we are always at the preliminaries, just as they are all that remains in memory.

In so far as a man's[39] sexual history provides a key to his life, it is because in his sexuality is projected his manner of being toward the world, that is, toward time and other men . . . Neither the body nor existence can be regarded as the original of the human being, since they presuppose each other . . . What is particularly important, is that when we say that sexuality has an existential significance or that it expresses existence, this is not to be understood as meaning that the sexual drama[40] is in the last analysis only a manifestation or a symptom of an existential drama. The same reason that prevents us from "reducing" existence to the body or to sexuality, prevents us also from "reducing" sexuality to existence: the fact is that existence is not a set of facts (like "psychic facts") capable of being reduced to others or to which they can reduce themselves, but the ambiguous setting of their inter-communication, the point at which their boundaries run into each other, or again their woven fabric.

*

When people act in sex, nowadays, they are half the time acting up. They do it because they think it is expected of them. Whereas as a matter of fact it is the mind which is interested, and the body has to be provoked.[41]

1

Lifting

Desire arises. It feels it, knows it. It knows that it is its own lifting up, its lifting away. Less an elevation or an erection than a movement up and away. Less, or better.

Desire is the knowledge of this movement. Of this transport. It is not turned toward a future or toward a goal to attain. If it seems possible to identify what is desired, it also knows that this does not constitute an endpoint. Desire knows that it has its end in itself: it is of desiring. It is also of self-interruption—in a happy or unhappy abandonment—because interruption belongs to the tension of desire just as the pause or the fall belongs to flight.

Desire sustains language and language sustains itself through desire: the one gives the other the élan of sense, which only takes place in the address, the appeal, the declaration, adoration, or exclamation. The speaking being is also the desiring being. It is desiring *also*—that is, in accord with the two facets of sense: signification and sending. Or rather, ideality and energy. No ideality (no concept, idea, sense in the common sense of the term) truly holds up (in truth) without being upheld, held by a force that carries it. This is obvious when it comes to saying "I love you, I desire you." But, in the final analysis, the same goes for all true speech, speech that even slightly overflows mere information ("hello" or "farewell" or a whole book of philosophy, a novel, a poem, as well as a conversation). The specificity of the speaking animal is not that it cuts itself off from the rest of living things to reside solely in language: no, this is not the way in which "poetically man dwells"! The speaking animal gives speech to the animal, which is entirely different.

> *Calla screamed and clutched at her lover so close against her she could not see his face, her eyes shut tight against his face as the huge man pumped his life's blood into her, groaning and burrowing helpless as a resentful child, "Uh-uh-uh," he moaned forcing her by painful little inches backward in the dirt until at last it was over . . .*[42]

In sex, this speech passes to its limits. It thereby feels itself in contact with the force of desire, while desire feels itself in the desire to be spoken. This passage to the limit can be presented thus: human sex does not speak, but it is a lyricist. It wants to set words to its music. To its tension, its force, its energy. The result is an unsolvable differend between speech and music. The history of the arts leaves no doubt about the preponderance of music. Music carried the day because its victory carried into the religious veneration of the text. This veneration was itself dispersed by its own movement pushing it toward the transport of the word into divine music. Augustine said that singing is praying two times: but the second time renders the first in vain.

Sex the lyricist is unceasingly compelled to drive its songs, operas, and operettas — even up to its *Sprechgesang* — back to an ultimate vibration where speech turns itself into the echo of its own limit. Bawdy songs only go so far: wordless music has always outdone them. Nevertheless, the urge to say, to name the transport of a "kiss whoever you want" continues to haunt — unnoticed, in less ribald guise — "serious" song and music (*Tristan and Isolde, Pelléas and Mélisande, Lulu,* Berio's music for voice, etc.). The same goes for images and visual arts, but monstration withdraws from transport (even as it sustains a secret whispering of names, the murmur of "Sex, there it is. Look").

In any event, the song knows when to keep quiet: "What the fourth did / Is not said in this song." (This famous song, it must be recalled, because it refers to raising up and uprising, first appeared in a comic opera from 1789.)[43]

There is nothing to see and nothing to say. But there is a lifting of rhetoric and timbre. A lifting away — a ravishment — of a touch.

2

Transmission

Language and sex come together from far off and lift each other away, raise each other up far into the distance. They form the double aspect of a relation that, at the origin, separates being-in-itself from itself, or being closed upon its nothingness from itself; and that sends it far off, toward its own disappearance — silence and *jouissance*, effusion, joy, and loss.

They are two modes of address, sending, destination: sense. The relation between them forms nothing other than the play of sense, its opening, its space. It goes from one to the other and only thus does each become real, actual. Each act of speech desires an absolute of existence — "I say: 'a flower'. . . ." — and each desire for sex touches on an absolute existence. Which can only occur, each time, by sending to the other and into the other.

Otherness, here, is not a matter of altruism: the other

bores a black hole into the Same, a massive compactness deprived of all presence; for, in order to present itself, presence must *come*. And in order to come it must be sent, addressed, expedited. This is what is called existence: the coming of everything to everything. Of every other/same to every same/other. Language makes everything come to the status of being addressed, presented: *look here—a flower!* Precisely, this utterance does not say "see," but rather "look at the form in truth," the idea. There is nothing to see. Sex brings an existence to the status of being addressed, stationed toward the other, in the other: *an enjoyment and/or a child*. Here, too, nothing to see. Here, too, is a truth.

The sense of the word, the sense of enjoyment, or the sense of having a child are a matter of lifting ever further off. Sense, properly speaking—that is, always improperly—inheres in its arising, its uprising, its rebellion against any requirement to abide or to signify. This is how sense is double—both sensible and intelligible, not as the double regime of an incompatible opposition but, on the contrary, as the necessary division whereby each interrupts the other. Language and sex mutually intercut one another. The first defies the other to say itself, the second defies the first to do itself.

Sense is said in order to be done and is done in order to be said. It does not only inhere in the sending of existents to one another: this sending—this liftoff, this raising up—always expedites itself outside of itself. Just as there is no "being," there is no "with." Herein arises the formidable ambivalence and ambiguity of everything that pertains to the *com*: communication, commerce, copula (which consists of *co* plus *apio*, to link). The "with" is never a thing, a substance, or a subject. It is the element of sense alone, in all of its senses—that is, in all the ways of sensing, of receiving, or of repulsing an outside, of not being "inside" without this outside that comes and that distances itself.

On the one side, there is the friction of sexual coming-and-going, the caress, the approach, the parade: the other is occupied by the friction of words, the departure-return of speech acts, the translation of languages, and their untranslatability. Not to mention the two significations that Latin idioms offer of the word *tongue*.

This is where the grand affair of the "mind" and the "body" plays itself out. It does not play out between envelope and contents, but rather between two aspects or modes of the same disposition to sense that is at once that of the communication of life and of the transmission of truth — or of truth as transmission.

3

Appropriation

Language and sex make truth of one another: that is, an interruption of sense. Suspension of continuity, discontinuity as point of apparition. An other (s/he) of the other appears: outside immanence, outside being-in-itself, an outside that authorizes, opens the possibility of an inside that is only a place of emission, sending, raising.

Interruption and relaunch. New demand: say to me, do to me. Say what you do, do what you say. This is the double exigency of desire, the double imperative whose gap, we also know, cannot be reduced. Making love is "impossible" because it does not pertain to the possible.[44] The possible is only ever what can be represented with the help of the already given. The impossible is thus what cannot be represented in this manner and must be renounced. These two eventualities hang upon the schema of the realization of an available representation (which comes down to speaking of the action of the will, which is precisely supposed to possess the power to put its representations into effect).

Language and sex, in turn, both part of one another and divided, do not proceed from a representation endowed with its own faculty of actualization. They do not proceed from a will but from desire. Desire does not pertain to power. It tends toward itself—or toward infinity: from the first, it carries unto the real of its act. With each word desire in language realizes the presentation of its truth: "a flower," "I desire you," "Hello!" This is neither possible nor impossible. It is simply real—vertiginously so because this real immediately gets carried away in the interminable and impetuous course of sense (what did I say? Did I *mean* to say it or was it said from elsewhere? And what? etc.).

The reality of this real lifts toward the real "itself," its idea, its true form, the thing (*res*). The thing is only what it is in presenting itself.

The desire for sex is the same. Indeed, the distinctive mark of such desire, with respect to other sensible appetites, from which, at the same time, it cannot be separated, is that it isn't directed toward an object. The object of desire is always in excess of the object—that is, of anything appropriable. Desire lifts toward the inappropriable, thus always unappropriated and inappropriate. Toward what does not gather itself up. The ontological tenor of desire is a movement outside of self, a lifting away. For some time now, desire is what gives a name and a form to an elementary movement of thought engaged by the departure of the gods: the élan toward the "divine" or the "without-god" of an infinitely open world—with, of course, all the chances and risks that pertain to an unlimited opening.

Language and sex entered a regime of infinitude when their sacred character was effaced; that is, when sense is no longer transmitted as an original repository given in language and in semination: when it remains to come, to be done, and to be invented. Instead of being received and transmitted, language and sex, from now on, have to be found, which means to be desired, because they are found as the élan or as the thrust of sense. That is, as address. There where this élan passes from hes and shes to others, it also addresses itself toward an alterity that must itself be sought out. All sacrality is not thereby abolished, of course: it is regained as what remains inappropriable within alterity. Or as a permanent and constitutive alteration: what is addressed alters itself, the play of speech sets off, gets lost, and sets off again on its own, the sense of generation disseminates lineages even while it disseminates its own thrust that is desired for itself. The most appropriated is the inappropriable.

Language and sex desire one another without thereby forming subjects. Each relates to itself without consisting in anything other than this relation. A subject perhaps occurs there where the two intersect: a point where sex is named (presented) and where language is engendered as proper (I speak "in my name"). This punctual intersection, always put back into play, does not prevent the double élan of sense from preceding every subject and succeeding all of them.

4

Fiction

To enjoy: to be carried away. To escape oneself, to let go of oneself, to be taken up in letting go. To receive this escape itself as an encounter with the other escape (*"desire that trembled to meet desire,"* Conrad Aiken). The jouissance of language is the passage from one word into another, from one phrase to the other, escaping itself and trembling to meet itself (*"Let your verse be what goes soaring, sighing, / Set free, fleeing from the soul gone flying,"* Paul Verlaine[45]). Sexual jouissance comes through the skin, exchanges outside for inside, trembles to feel itself fade away, meets on the fly. What these *jouissances* have in common, their crossing between call and sigh, is not satisfaction: it is rather stupefaction. The stupor of a flight that slips between presence and absence, between being and nonbeing.

Interruption of continuity — of linkage, of the transmission between each other and each other with the transport of both in the same element: a suspense, a separation that is no more isolation than fusion. A certain confusion — of identity, of signification, comprising both "pleasure" and "pain," because it is sharp, incisive. Shudder, spasm: contraction of a relay, an always primary and never complete throw. Emission of a signal of emission: a throw [*lancée*], the lifting [*levée*] of nothing but a throw, a lifting. Exclamation: *ah!* — which has no other sense than surprise and desertion. I let sense drop, the cord of sense. It passes through me as through you, indistinctly distinct. It distinguishes itself from everything and it distinguishes us together in a point outside of us. This point makes sense — as an unheard of yet expected speech.

For sex desires to be said. It desires itself said, named, designated. And yet, it cannot become said except by fiction because its point is found — bursts — outside of language and outside of bodies. It wishes to be figured, to take figure there where it's without figure. There, it must be said, where figure is abolished to the point of repulsing itself, even as it is equated with the face or the whole body.

Baubo exposing herself to Demeter opens her vulva up so high it becomes her chin. An African phallus bears a face on its shaft where the glans separates. Courbet's *Origin of the World*, deprived of a face, looks at us with the very thin pink slit between the lips of the vulva.

This infiguration forms fiction. It gazes at us; it envisages us and stares at us as the invention of itself. It speaks and pronounces: "I am not a woman, I am a world." Just as a voice intones to Flaubert's Saint Anthony.

We must imagine an ithyphallic figure that would pronounce: "I am not a man, I am a world." But Picasso said that the erect, virile member is as difficult to represent as the sun: his only attempt yielded just a funny little drawing. Erection, unto itself, verges on the grotesque as in Rimbaud's such joyous and harsh verses: *"Ithyphallic and solderish / Their jeerings have depraved it!"*[46]

Later we will return to the difference between being in the world and being world. For the moment, let's stay with the world. It is indeed the world that is figured, configured, and fictioned by language and sex. A world: a circulation of the ones to the others, a commerce of sense with interminable transactions and negotiations all of whose points of emission, reception and dispersion determine infinity in action. From a mouth to an ear, from a breath to a breath, from skin to skin, and from lip to lip—in every sense and every direction, the double flux of the desire to make a world. The desire to trace each passage that desire inscribes, each all-to-itself as an unto-all, and inversely. And this can only happen through circulation, departure and return, grasping and letting go, concretion and liquefaction, retraction and outpouring, in touch bit by bit with all things.

To make oneself world: to respond to the very fact of existing. Because this fact, unto itself, as the fact of the ex-, claims its rights—that is, its sense. Which is to make a world. To be world and to be in the world. To be configured: to figure to one another and each to himself. To say one another [*se dire*] and to touch one another [*se toucher*]. To exist one another [*s'exister*].[47]

5

Real

The world is the fiction, the confection, the presentation and the configuration of the bit-by-bit of all things. The spacetime of monads each of which relays to all the others. This fiction is nowise a feint: it is the realization of the real. Reality is not a given, it gives itself. It is not posited, it posits itself. It is not found, it finds itself. "It was found by itself, just like that . . ."[48] Once again, before any subject, in an autonomy that does not return to self but sends itself out, exposes itself, presents itself. And only obeys the movement of coming to presence. Here you go.

Here you go: this is an expression and a gesture. The thing presents itself as such. As thing—that is, as a real that gives itself. And that gives this gift, that transmits it. Language avers the infinity of the gift because it cannot be signified as such: there is neither donor nor donee. There is no sense of sense. Sex avers infinity as the real that traverses me, giving itself outside (as "nature," "life").[49]

Outside language and sex there is transformation: all of the evolutions, explosions or expansions, and technologies, of course, and their way of pursuing the gift without reason or end. But, first of all, there is the transformation on the basis of which sex and then language came to configure what we call "sense" in all the senses of the word—that is, according to the permanent change of words into one another and things or (masculine and feminine) beings by one another, into one another. This transformation is what we name the universe and, in it, nature, or life. It is nothing other than the fact that "it gives itself," "it presents itself," "it comes."

Transformation is enervated by desire: when it happens to

furnish an animal with speech, it opens a new configuration, inaugurates another fiction that transforms itself in turn. Having no reason or principle, transformation also has no ultimate end. It ceaselessly produces ends and goes beyond them—but language and sex indicate something other, a finality without end.

No need to go back in time to envisage existence in terms of the desire for sense that it *is* (because it is its being much rather than a passion or a motion). It is only necessary to turn, in all simplicity, to the upsurge of the world. To the *ex nihilo* that isn't a magic operation but the upsurge without reason of what is, of what gives itself and might then supply itself with reasons and ends as well as exceed them—that can return *in nihilum* without intention or foresight. *Nothing* provides the only measure whereby anything can gain sense because, otherwise, sense would already be given; it would not be given as the desire that manifestly it awakens.

This desire for sense occurs as the possibility that the upsurge itself will come, in a certain way, to meet itself: *ex nihilo* enacts itself many times, and perhaps in many heterogenous ways (giving itself other forms of "life" or "thought," other universes). It re-enacts itself, in any event, with life, with a multiplicity of living forms among which it re-enacts itself once again in sexuated reproduction, and then with speaking animality. Each time the *nothing* is what is realized anew according to a lesson that must always be repeated—that "nothing" is nothing other than the thing itself, *res*, from which the French noun *rien* derives, which designates something that is nothing—any old thing, insignificant, a detail, a trifle—and that only becomes "no thing" when it is itself negated ("it's nothing").

In Shakespearean English, *thing* colloquially designated sex (the organ of either sex). Sometimes it designated the penis whereas *nothing* designated the vulva (or a boy's anus). In

Hamlet, Ophelia plays with this sense of the word. In *Othello*, Emilia says to Iago, "I have a thing for you" (3.3.302)—the handkerchief—and he takes it as a sexual invitation.

Nothing, then, the minimal thing, infinitesimal and intimate being in an imminence, in a pressing urgency. The real that imposes itself and calls itself forth at the same time: that *is* not without calling itself to be. Which is in its coming, in its lifting. Nihilism has its inverse: the flipside of "the will to will" that wants to increase its power over all things, exactly coextensive with this power, is desire lifted toward itself as an opening, an address without destination, a simply suspended salutation.

Desire not as "being," if this is understood as a substantive or substantial denomination, but rather merely as the progressive form of a verb[50]—*to be*—that cannot at all be reduced to the "copula deprived of spirit" that Hegel invoked (copula primed to be re-absorbed into the dialectic of the subject and the attribute) but rather that unfolds itself and stretches itself out as existence, exposure to nothing other than the coexistence, the conjunction, and even the copulation of all things—none of these terms, in turn, reducible to a substance, a subject, or an object.

Perhaps we live in a time when the inanity of the production of power disposes itself either to get lost in the interminable (potential infinity) or to flip into an address or salutation such as: "look here!" (actual infinity). A flower, you or me, sometimes us, an image, a contact, a cadence, a life-and-death. A dispatch detached from the hope for ultimate ends and measurable values. A way to evaluate the incalculable, the inestimable gift without giver or receiver: the gift that existence itself gives to itself, between coming and lifting away, each time alone and exposed to every other one.

If this is what it is—not much but a whole new departure *ex nihilo*[51] (and I say "a departure" and not "a beginning" because the latter implies a programmed sequence whereas a departure goes and comes with each step), as well as an inversion of nihilism without the production of new idols — then it is worth thinking anew the real of language and sex — or rather, how we address one another.

6

History

We know that Michel Foucault discerned in modernity a will to unveil sex, to bring to light a secret that belongs essentially to sex (similar to that of madness). In this unveiling he saw the formation of a power of repression and control as the same time as the possibility of a new use of pleasure.

Identifying Christianity as the origin of the desire in the permanent, unlimited, and hyperbolic form that will have preoccupied so-called Western thought up to the present, Foucault inverted a dominant perspective. This inversion doesn't only concern sex. It must be understood that the entire phenomenon in question entails a general mutation that can be called existential — but in the sense that it comprises all the known forms of existence, human or otherwise. After having aligned the meaning of being with the infinity, an infinity designated as "love," and after having extracted the meaning of being from the representation of a subject-object of love (notated as "God," or else "dayrise"), our history passed through a stage of forcefully marked sexual character.

The first signs of this stage appeared in the 18th century. What will be called "emancipation" is presented at the same time in social, economic, political, and sexual modalities. The 19th century, flanked early by two emblematic figures of sex as law, principle, and end — the figures of Sade and Fourier—pursued what had been the libertine "indiscretion" into scientific investigation and into what emerges between Nietzsche and Freud under the name of *Trieb* (which the French translated as *pulsion* after eschewing *instinct*, to which, on their side, the English preferred *drive*). With *Trieb* and with the never settled question of its translation, they penetrated into a virgin domain that, it must indeed be said, is none other than the ancient domain of the divine or the sacred.

Trieb had been, in particular, the term that Kant used to designate reason's inherent tension toward the unconditional—or toward what, not dependent on anything, imposes itself absolutely but cannot be constituted as an object of knowledge. This tension produces the pseudo-objects of metaphysics, which must be renounced in favor of the tension itself that presents itself (without allowing itself to be objectified) as the freedom of initiative (the creation of ends), as universal duty (to treat everyone as an end) and as finality without end (creation of forms for themselves). If examined closely, this triple character—each element of which itself is unpresentable otherwise than as a postulate or a form of regulative fiction—clearly reprises in its own fashion the features of Christian love detached from their reference to a supposed divine subject-object of love. But the subject-object of the tension still remains cast in the same mold because, in the name of the "person," it tends to become confused with the tension itself.

The human person is a person, someone, whoever and not a substance (individual, character). Whether everything or nothing the random, insignificant thing is not an object but rather a point of relay from thing to thing. Double punctuation, double contact.

The thrust of Kantian reason in a certain manner opens a new regime *ex nihilo*, that of desire without object or subject, without beginning or end, entirely bound up with its own tension. Freud will ask: How does tension give pleasure? Without knowing it, he thereby posed the question of the new *ex nihilo*: how can a tension without the prospect of slackening still give pleasure by itself? "To give pleasure"— that is, to desire to persevere in the reality of its tension? In this real that is, in short, unrealizable?

All of the rationalized curiosities, the portraits of sexual psychopathologies and ribald popular tales, spicy debaucheries and feverish languor that impassioned an epoch are plunged, as derisory symptoms, into this new figure of the metaphysical or divine abyss. The invention of psychoanalysis and of the "unconscious" is only a collateral effect, modeled upon an objective scientificity and a therapy,[52] of a wholly different revelation in which sex operates a manifest junction with speech.

More than on couches, it is in literature, in art, and in revolution that sex speaks—and speech makes itself sexual. Simultaneously, a major transformation occurs, that of an entire social and technical praxis which desires to recreate the world, desire's own speaking out and language's desire not to say but to make love. Two of verses by Sergei Yesenin, from 1925, say it all:

> *Let kisses become kisses,*
> *Your fingers, let them wander.*[53]

May the lips that speak be the lips that kiss, may the mouths that kiss be mouths that speak, may breaths mix their exhalations and their spirits, may tongues be said as they swirl around one another in the confluence of saliva, may the poem wander with the fingers: this is not mere beautification, not a literary ornament, but literally sex that speaks; it is the letter making itself flesh.

It will be said that the time for such speech has disappeared into a transformation of kissing into orgy or orgasm, into the bulimia of sexologies and of sex toys, into the miserable ambivalence between a jouissance that consumes itself and a jouissance that abandons itself. It will be added that speech and the letter are thereby transformed into linguistic debauchery, into verbal complacency, and into self-proclaimed and self-consumed significance. Consensus about all this is presumed amidst a general consensus about the catastrophic direction of our history, cozied up to the inverse consensus among those who imagine themselves devotees of the exponential jouissance of interminable dominations and satisfactions. Nonetheless, we know quite well that consensus is always suspect. It is produced by the refusal to endure complexity, undecidability, and the imminence of the impossible. In fact, it seeks to avoid suffering. But there is no such thing, precisely, as sexual consensus. None whatsoever. Every desire must be borne or renounced. This is what eroticist euphoria, already disintegrating, thinks it can dissimulate . . .

The lieutenant handed him a list of persons sentenced to execution, and the colonel signed it without even a glance.

Afterward he told the adjutant to sit down on the edge of the bed and began to stroke his rosy cheeks.
"You pretty boy," he lisped with his toothless mouth.

The lieutenant flushed deeply as the baron pulled him close with his scrawny arms. Again the baron felt himself the Roman patrician.[54]

7

Technics and Transcendence

Nothing, indeed, is less certain than consensus. Too pregnant, it bears witness most often to a reflex rather than a reflection. Not only does it offer false affirmations: its truth is that of the symptom. We don't like it when secret sex is exhibited, when communicative language becomes obscure and silent. However, it is not certain that this is the ground of things—to the extent that there can be a ground.

Sex has always been sacralized in one manner or another. Social cults and rules bear abundant witness to this fact. Language has always been what Valéry calls "holy language": apophasis, verbal magic, and poetry show it in every culture. Not by chance, in both sex and language we rediscover indices of sacrality. And what if we were not in the process of desacralization, as so many people have repeated, but rather of discovering a wholly other experience? The sacred has always been constituted of another presence, withdrawn but effective, dangerous and attractive because it is the presence of what relates us to ourselves as beings in excess of ourselves.

Existence is the name of this excess as soon as it is designated as ours—that is, within us or through us the upsurge of the immeasurable, the inappropriable, everything that we name in negative or subtractive terms, as if lacking any other possibility of designation. Indeed, we have no names to say what pertains to another property than what we call "nature" and "man." Between the two, or rather, beyond their distinction, unfolds a regime that we call "technics" and that seems to take the place of all possible appropriations—mastery, the setting of goals, the production of goods (in the full scope of the term). And it seems to us that, inside this regime, our own relation to ourselves is transformed into technique: notably, into the technique of sex (both with respect to the reproduction of the species and with respect to jouissance) and the technique of language (which would subject itself to the transmission of always verifiable information, regulated by procedures of conformity not to linguistic but rather numerical and calculable facts).

Sex and language, however, form the double element according to which we exist as the "human species"—which is to say, as the species that, in the one way or the other, exceeds any given order, any order determined by a model of what, we believe, is stabilized by the orders and laws of a cosmic, natural, and living universe. But what comes to the fore, today, thanks to us and as us in our own existence, is that our technics overturns these orders and these laws, not always transforming them but at least enlisting them into the regime of this technics.

An assertion becomes inevitable: it is from this supposed nature and its presumed order, in fact, that the human species arises with its properties of language and enjoyment. Language excepts itself from all orders of communication between living beings and human sex excepts itself from all orders of the reproduction of species. In both cases, the exception consists in the fact that the function, of language or of sex, takes itself for an end in itself at the same time as it operates as a means of communication or reproduction.

Taking itself as an end, the function no longer functions in the same manner. The exception is excessive. Nonetheless, it emerges from nature and from life. For quite a long time, technics was understood—which also means conceived and practiced—as a fundamentally natural means of supplementing certain of the human animal's insufficiencies. For Aristotle, there could only be a limited number and type of technologies in each domain, which, it must be understood, was more or less achieved in Aristotle's time. But technology has not ceased to exceed limits and to exceed itself. Has it thereby become any less "natural"? The question makes no sense.

Nowhere does "Nature" occur in a "natural" state. Human beings have not always been there; but when they arrive the nature within them humanizes itself—that is, displaces itself in a new way. What was originally a movement without principle or goal—energy, turbulence, clinamen, life and death, metabolisms, evolutions, circumvolutions, mutations—is now expressed as such: as sense always being born (*nasco, natura*) and always disappearing (silence, sigh, spasm).

The only thing that has sense is the reflection whereby technology unfolds nature—in a singular mode, certainly, because it implies the renewed opening of an *ex nihilo*. The human species, then, pursues the natural course of things—to the extent that it remains possible to use such an expression. Accordingly, the mutations and revolutions of technology pursue the same course.

> In the spring this giant thicket, untrammeled behind
> its iron gate and four walls, went on heat in the
> universal labor of seeding and growth, trembled in
> the warmth of the rising sun like an animal which
> breathes the scent of cosmic love.[55]

The "natural" course of things comes with a denaturation or a transnaturation. In this sense, although the "transhumanism" that dreams of sort of human supernature might understand itself as a transformation, or even a transgression, it actually belongs to the course of things. This does not mean, however, that this course is oriented in a certain direction or proceeds at a constant or accelerated speed. It signals, rather, that the emergent forms of excess, leaps or ruptures—such as steam, electricity, the atom, and informatic circuits constitute both interlinked stages and a mere succession without determinate progression (despite advances in power, speed, and discriminating capacities).

Emergences, events also occur in the technical course of social organizations, the representations and relations between members of the transformative species *par excellence*,

between this species and itself, between itself and its presumed nature (and nature as such). The latter is by essence
transhuman, or transcendent. *Transumanar*, as we know,
comes from Dante, who cannot not have had the verb "to
transcend" in mind, and, consequently, cannot not have situated his poem in rivalry with theology.

Technology is transcendence: this scandalous proposition is necessary to grasp something of the real that comes
to us when a history sheds any appearance of ultimate progress (on the model of natural growth) in order to indicate its
own transgression or its own transcendence. Immanence—a
vaunted word at the present moment—merely signifies that
transcendence takes place right at existence, our existence
as the existence in which every existent is at stake (not excluding the possibility that other games are being played at
the same time unbeknownst to us).

8

Excessive Nature

Under these conditions, what is to be done with the "sexual
liberation" that emerges as ethical debauchery and anthropological peril? What is to be done with signification that is
unverifiable ("poetic" or "thinking") and does not rely upon
positive knowledge?

The two situations are correlative but not equivalent or
homogenous. From this point onward, for reasons of economy and clarity, I will follow the first and won't attempt in
any systematic way to join up with the second. Later in this
book, or perhaps in another book, I will return to their conjunction.

The gap is manifest: sex can be found in the vast majority

of living species, while it is difficult to discern modes of animal communication as continuous with one another as those found in speaking animality. The difference among animal and human sexual organs is not comparable to the differences among their phonatory organs. Of course, birds and mammals communicate using sound and other elements (which also goes for human beings), but human phonation is organized differently—just as, let it be said merely in passing for now, the conditions of human vision and olfaction (upright stance) affect human sexuality.

Sex is present in human beings in an animal continuity comparable, if not identical, to that of the great vital functions—respiration, nutrition, and defecation. This is a major reason to be interested in sex, whether or not one wishes to respect its secret or to drag this secret into the open. The vital functions modulate the relationship of the living being with the outside: they make the living into a system open to the outside because it remains relatively closed upon an inside whose "interiority" consists precisely in making possible exposure to an outside and ongoing exchanges with it. In this sense, life is *ek-sistence* in its principle and its essence. Life is already outside itself, hungry for itself and in excess of itself—to the point of seeking its death.[56]

With reproduction, life perpetuates and renews the multiplicity of "individuals" that can be defined as units of exchange with the outside in which other individuals take part. Life is not simply outside of itself: its being is to be outside. Because life itself emerges from nonliving matter, such matter cannot be thought without this eventuality or without this possibility of emergence—this remarkable point of *ex nihilo*—because complexification, of any kind, from which life emerges, does not produce what it authorizes: an auto-affected, relational, feeding, and reproductive living being that arises in and from the nothing-living (which is, however, not dead, of course, nor even inert).

Sex arises in life as a supernumerary function: it is not necessary to reproduction. Certain contemporary biologists confirm that the increase in diversification by the sexual process (division of chromosomes, recombinations and mutations, etc.) do not necessarily explain the fact of sexuality, which might well contribute to the stabilization of the species while, inversely, non-sexuated reproduction is not incapable of diversification. In any event, sex plays the greatest role in the reproduction of living beings and mobilizes immense energy within them through the profusion of morphologies, behaviors, and ecstasies. Rutting, this word that mainly designates sexual roaring or wailing, is feverish, ardent, and noisy. Even in nonspeaking animals, it can give rise to nonreproductive sexual acts, masturbation without hands, by rubbing, or even by exposure to the wind as Andalusian mares have been observed to do.

All of this is familiar but hasn't yet been thought on the level of a civilization stripped of sacred reference points. Where the gods are or were animal figures, there, too, the existence of the world, of life and of sex itself refers, in one way or another, to a mythical sexuality, generative of generation itself. When Freud writes that the drives are our myths, he indicates very precisely that in the *trieben* we can formulate our reason for being—or recount our own history, fiction for ourselves what demands to be figured: the reason for being without reason, existing as such. The *trieben*, however, is the thrust, the drive as élan, setting into motion, penchant, growth, ascent, something on the order of the *vigor* that constitutes the primary sense of the Latin *vegere* from which the word *vegetable* sprouted. The drive, in sum, speaks life before life, an archelife [*archivie*] that leaves no archive [*archive*] because it only takes place by emerging from nothing and for nothing, emerging to emerge. Each word here is too much because it emerges from nothing, from the thing to the extent that it drives itself by itself to be.

The Kantian drive of reason, the desire for the unconditional is nothing other than the thrust turning toward itself
and coming to know itself as constitutive excess. Reason is
nature—natality, being born, birthing pushing itself toward
its own unconditionality. That is to say, toward its absoluteness: delinked from everything, not capable of being linked
to anything, capable of not being anything but being born
[*pouvant* n'étre *que* naître].

Excess, transcendence, transgression, and birth here do
not postdate a pregiven condition, an established measure,
an immanence, a law, or an origin: the origin is the arising or the lifting up (*orior*) that nothing precedes, not even
night. This arising or lifting inaugurates the separation of
days and nights, the luminous and the obscure. This origin
is not inscribed at a point; it is produced in and as its own
tension, in the rhythm it beats, its pulsation. It does not have
an identity; it differs from itself; it differs itself, rises up and
sends itself off as the spacetime of its lifting, as the event
of its coming. It doesn't begin or end; its only being is the
self-divergence of everything that exists: the distancing, the
alteration, the sending. "Being" as sending to an outside is
definitely—as I have already suggested above—at least one
aspect of what Heidegger sought to designate this side of and
beyond the ontologies of being as given (or giving) being; of
what Derrida sought to mark as the *différance* of and in the
origin.

That the thing exceeds itself—differs itself, transcends
itself, transgresses itself—in principle; that nature exceeds
itself in technology; and that technology exceeds itself in an
anthropological mutation that has hardly begun, this is what
we experience as desire.

Difference differentiates itself, defers itself, engages a differend: not by chance, it is actually a matter—very simply,
thus vertiginously—of what is neither posited, nor placed,

of what does not subsist in itself. It is a matter of what is—if it "is"—only in élan, happenstance, tension, drive. No philosophy, no theology, no poetry, nor even any science has ever halted its positing of substances, subjects, identities. No treatise of the One since Plato's *Parmenides* has ever been anything other than problematic or aporetic.

What about Parmenides himself? Even as he affirmed the indivisible unity and continuity of being, he still says: "Everything holds together: what is approaches what is [or "holds close," since the verb is *pelazô*, which can also have a sexual meaning]." And Parmenides says that the *daimon* that governs everything pushes or propels the female and the male toward one another—adding that Eros is the very first among the gods.

Moravia writes: "Desire, in reality, is no more than nature's decisive, powerful aid to something that existed before her and without her. It was the hand of nature, drawing from the womb of the future—the human, moral child—of things to come."[57] It is not certain that these "things to come" must be "human and moral" except in the sense of an unlimited transgression or transcendence of what these words seem to enclose. What's certain is that so-called nature, in its pulsating power, arrives from far outside of nature, before and after it—even if and definitely most of all if this excess is nothing "more" or nothing "other," not a "supernature," nothing other than the being-born [*le naître*] of nature in its arising, in its sending off, its throw and its coming (the whole complex of values comprised by the great Akkadian and Greco-Latin family to which this word is bound, along with the Greek *gigno*). Nothing other: the other itself, the other at the heart of the same as its very desire. Being-born [*le naître*] as not being [*n'être*] anything other than one's own alteration and *enjoying* as the experience of being thereby altered in one's being.

9

Desire

Desire obviously does not emerge from sex but rather sex from desire. In such a way, however, that sex is less an effect or an instrument of desire than its incarnation, its presence at the heart of existence. It is not a matter of reducing existence to sex—as so many once believed they could reproach Freud for having done—but rather, inversely, of discerning in sex the distinctive traits of existence. Which is to say, something other than a "natural" or "animal" characteristic—and more precisely, as we have just seen, another characterization of what is called "nature" and "animal" (without thus definitively omitting either the "mineral" or the "vegetable").

Not by chance has eros suffused the entire history of philosophy after having played all of the sacred roles it's known for. It presented itself with the force of attraction that, in Empedocles, begins to gather far flung members scattered at random and which, become a body, come to desire one another. It presents itself with divine Eros in Plato, the furious excitement of the lover, which, he suggested, would be even more intense if it could turn not only toward sensible beauty but toward *phronesis*—that is, in this thinker, thinking itself less as intellection than as active tension, itself desirous.

From Plato to Hegel, from Nietzsche to us, desire has always shown itself to be the desire of desire. The fact that, for a long time, it was diverted into the desire for knowledge—a distinctive trait of our culture—should not make us ignore that in knowledge itself a desire abides: the desire for true knowledge is the desire for knowledge that knows itself knowing and that thus infinitely enjoys itself in the manner of Hegel's "absolute knowledge." This knowledge, indeed, is similar in this respect to Spinoza's "intellectual love" as well as to the infinite self-overcoming of science in Husserl—only to cite two possible examples. There is no knowledge that does not desire self-knowledge: this is the regime of logos. "Know thyself" does not command us to be self-conscious in the usual sense of this expression but rather to know oneself as knowing and consequently as able to relate to oneself as an object of one's own knowledge, an object that, in turn, cannot be posited but must make itself the subject of the gap whereby it diverges from itself in order infinitely to return to itself.

When Spinoza affirms that "beatitude is not the reward for virtue but virtue itself," he affirms virtue as *virtus*, the active force of what he calls "divine love," which alone enables us to gain true knowledge, which is knowledge of infinity in act. Beatitude is thus itself an action and a tension. It is the spiritual name for a *jouissance* (but Spinoza also uses the verb *gaudere*) that is not a fulfillment but a renewed élan. Going further, Spinoza adds: "We do not enjoy beatitude because we keep our carnal desires in check. On the contrary, it is because we enjoy beatitude that we are able to keep our carnal desires in check."[58] What's at stake is desire through and through: if the desires of the flesh prevent us from gaining access to intellectual love, this love alone, the desire for divine knowledge that alone knows itself by itself along with the truth of the world, has the ability to master such desires and to submit them to its own elevation. In other words, this submission is more a matter of ascension than of contention. The struggles of the flesh are nothing other than its aspiration or its sublimation toward a superior regime.

Sublimation . . . this Freudian term remains quite obscure, even for Freud himself. The drive would change its sexual and/or aggressive aim (or both together) into a more spiritual, artistic, or intellectual goal. But changing the goal does not change the energy in play. Nietzsche had already understood that the artist's energy is sexual (without speaking of sublimation). One might also consider the possibility that sexual desire arises from the incarnation of a theoretical or aesthetic desire. Freud himself affirms that the idea of the beautiful presumes the impossibility of considering the genital organs as beautiful. Beauty would make it possible to surmount an aversion or a fear of sex as much as it would arise from the spiritualizing assumption of sexual appetite.

In one sense or another, it is always precisely a matter of the body and the spirit. The drive—desire, thrust, address—passes from one to the other. It makes and it forms this passage. Which is it, then? It is the passage from the inside to the outside, very exactly. The inside only occurs after the fact, as the retraction of the élan that opens the outside. The voice, the gesture, and the gaze carry out into the open in order to form—one might say, to perform—nothing other than this opening itself and with it a relation, a distance and a proximity with other openings. In this sense, there is a profoundly sensible (aesthetic) intimacy between sex and the arts: they modulate the desire by which bodies wish to feel what they are, bodies in the world or even body-worlds. The arts do this through distinct forms, sex through the tendency to render forms indistinct.

> *The human sexes are both also single eyes wide open.*
> *Each sex that desires is a single eye which opens and, for the other sex, a single eye that petrifies, that hypnotizes the-other-who-desires-back-in-order-to-open-back.*
> *Which dilates and pries open the eye of the vulva that it doesn't see and into which it penetrates.*[59]

Desire in all its vicissitudes and energies is the desire of desire—that is, the expansion of being as the very essence of "being" or "existing." How not to represent it, confusedly as one inevitably does, as a blind or brilliant thrust at every point of existence, at every place and every moment of the world (and also, just as well, spread over its totality)?

In the speaking animal, desire signals itself to itself. It carries itself tangibly and expressly to the extremity of its motion and its emotion—that is, to an excess that culminates in its own vanishing. Spasm and silence.

10

Continuous, Discontinuous

Quite obviously, the thrust of the drive has no place, no time, and no support. It takes place everywhere and nowhere, like the very upsurge of each thing, similar to what Descartes called continuous creation. The idea of continuous creation does not contradict that of a creation that is unique and outside of time. It is even possible to find theologies that suggest as much. To take place outside of time and at each instant is not contradictory. The *ex nihilo* is always available, even if, of course and above all, the *nihil* is understood as an overcoming of being rather than a nothingness (for which it is also possible to find theologico-philosophical attestations). Which signifies: even if *nothing*, the thing or the coexistence of things, always carries from the outset and by itself beyond pure position unto exposition. One could also say: there is no position that is not exposed. Accordingly, there is no presence that does not come—or withdraw—from its pure and simple posited identity (supposing that such a thing exists . . .). Even a stone outstrips its inertia, carried upon a planet, at the bottom of a stream, or out among imperceptible gusts of air.

The continuity of being or beings is what's primarily at stake in erotism as Bataille understands it in his book by that name—certainly the most penetrating reflection on this theme so far.[60] The first sentence of the book pronounces: "Erotism, it may be said, is assenting to life to the point of death."[61] Death, Bataille writes later, "means continuity of being."[62] Life, in reproducing itself, introduces a discontinuity. Death, on the contrary, would be identical to being equal to itself in a plenitude and a simple boundlessness. Erotism wishes to replace the isolation of beings with "feeling of profound continuity."[63]

Desire can be considered as desire for such continuity because it is the movement that urges an existence toward others in accordance with the thrust that makes it exist. Undoubtedly, the lover can "perceive the depth of being" in the beloved. Undoubtedly as well, the lover and the beloved—each being both the one and the other—are thus impelled to desire the enjoyment of this "perception" to such excess that they would each disappear with the other and into the other. If desire is the desire of desire, the renewal of its own inevitably hyperbolic excess, losing itself in the very élan that carries it, it represents, in sum, the culmination of the rapture [emportement] or the trans-port that constitutes it. However, it never reaches such a point. Or, it might reach it but only in the mode of nothing . . . "Sex is so nothing,"[64] people say after Bataille and after Warhol (to whom we will return) without really knowing who said it first—because, in some sense, it was everyone, an anonymous rumor weary of sex for sale.

For Bataille, erotism is bound to be nothing but a comedy, much like sacrifice, because lovers—one of the two at least, much like the sacrificer in the sacrifice—most often do not die. The word "comedy" can be understood—as Bataille himself did—in its most common sense, as derision. Erotism toils at a mimetism destined to fail. It is certainly necessary to speak about sexual failure. But it isn't located on the same plane if "comedy" names the vanity of any sexual relation, felicitous or infelicitous. Such comedy, too, must be understood otherwise, no matter what Bataille's precise text or thought might say.

If sex seeks continuity, it only ever seeks it or finds it in the form of discontinuity. Lovers wish to experience together a "feeling of profound continuity": "together"—a word that possesses a local, temporal, and emotive value—does not signify "indistinctly." Even while the partners seek to enjoy at the same time, this search does not prevent each one from wanting to feel this simultaneity on their own. The horizon of continuity is that of the loss of feeling and this loss—represented as death—is or would also be the end of relations.

This is not a matter of opposing factual necessities to the force of desire. It is right, entirely, that desire tends toward its own annihilation in a pleasure that is not contentment but the often searing, unbearable extremity of the drive's urge and deviance. It is right that annihilation (the will to a will that succeeds in renouncing itself) can be desired and sometimes engaged. It is also right to affirm that children—when reproduction is at stake—"are the death of the parents," as Hegel says. But continuity will always remain *con*-tinuity. It has only a sense and a place in connection, the concert or combination of discrete elements. Bataille frequently utilizes liquid images (the waves of the sea, for example)—and it is right that sex results in a sort of liquefaction (or liquidation) of interlaced bodies. Nonetheless, Bataille himself knows very well that "water within water," or simple immanence, is removed from the minimal requirement of existing: an upsurge, a distinctive uplift. Transcendence or transgression transcends or transgresses within immanence—which, definitively (or rather, to begin with) simply never took place.

This inflection, the only one that I wish to introduce into Bataille's thinking, might be articulated in a more expressive fashion if we start with other words. Bataille speaks of fusion, the desire for fusion. He thus enters into a vast discourse—mystical and amorous, religious and erotic. Fusion makes the fused elements disappear into a new element. The word "confusion" (which can be found on occasion in Bataille's work on erotism) suggests a different possibility: a fusion that does not resolve itself in a transubstantiation but rather consists in a lack of distinction among substances or subjects that remain distinct. The confusion of bodies in an embrace like the confusion of feelings in desire (which wants more than it wants) exceeds the contrast between continuous and discontinuous. In a sense, sex is doubtless always liable to confusion. Or rather, it is itself confusion, indecisive identity and poorly discernable difference. Identity and difference of continuity and discontinuity. In other words, "relation": that which is not "a being" or "a subject," nor thereby a quality or an action, but rather a coming of ones to others, a coming in which the ones and the others exceed one another. Like they do in language: strained to the limit of their sense.

Already in Plato fusion appears only as a hypothetical intervention by the divine blacksmith (Hephaestus proposes to the lovers to "dissolve and melt them together with the breath of the furnace"). But this fiction—comic, once again—does not prevent amorous "unity" from having the status of an encounter or embrace between two.

In any event, the fiction of divine fusion perfectly expresses the force of an élan. And this force only starts moving if it feels itself pushed toward its own absorption in a unity where it recognizes both its truth and its disappearance: its end, in both senses of the word, its life as much as its death. Discontinuity is the condition of life whose continuity is assured by death. Comedy is itself also a tragedy, but tragedy could be, along with comedy, a paradoxical truth of sex: we will return to this point later.

11

Devouring

Desire arises: it feels it, knows it, knows that it is confused with this arising, this lifting up and breaking away, this carrying off of being.

It knows itself carrying itself outside of itself. Or rather, the whole "self" is committed unto this carrying off. Desire desires itself but it is not a self. It is stronger than a self, stronger than itself. It is pushed, pushed by a thrust that is more ancient or more profound that anything which might figure a principle or an origin. With desire, a sudden growth is obscurely revealed, a spurt like a flame that flares up under a magnifying glass in the sun.

And this sun certainly came first. Certainly, heat came before life and friction came before heat and agitation came before friction. Everything might have kept boiling on, in a continuous effervescence, but there was an interruption, a suspense in which a living being set itself apart, another type of agitation, a tension across an entire membrane.

As a cell swallowed up other cells, perhaps it discovered a gain in richness, complexity. This cannibalism could have suggested sexual division, a manner of breaking apart in order to mix.

Suggested, you say? But to whom by whom?

I'll grant you it was not a suggestion. It happened, there

you go. Biologists are the ones who suggest this cannibal hypothesis.

They know well that desire devours. One mustn't forget, however, that along with its prey it devours the wild animal that it is itself. *Infelix media torreberis Aetna*, Ovid writes to his lover: you might be consumed by the flames of Etna.

In scissiparity, the cell makes itself disappear. In sexuality, it disappears into a part of itself that another divided cell can absorb and mix with its own substance. From this confusion, in turn, emerges a cell that separates from half of itself, allowing it to combine with another spawn of the same dissection. Desire desires itself and desires to be devoured by itself.

Devouring itself it renews itself and annihilates itself in the same movement. It consumes itself and is reborn from its ashes. From nothing, that is. Desire comes from nothing and seeks nothing: it is Being strained by its own alteration and the consumption of any position of being, any presence in favor of an address, any signification in favor of the gaping of sense.

Neither in jouissance nor in its transmission does desire join up with anything but its own blaze, its own devouring, its exhaustion, its extenuation. It only swells in order to thin out, to become outrageously slight and yet always strained—to the point where the filament breaks along with life and the link between desiring being and the world where it emerged.

Too often we separate or oppose needs, appetites, inclinations, and desires. Everything, in the final analysis, arises from a demand inherent to and coextensive with being. Or rather with "be-ing" if one replaces the substantive with a verb (as Heidegger proposes that we do in the least frequent but unquestionably the most convincing version of his deconstruction of ontology).

If one goes further and considers this verb, heedless of its grammar, as transitive (which Heidegger also proposes), the concept of being as *that which is* can be appreciably nudged toward the idea that *that which is*, no matter what it happens to be, is not "that" which it is in an attributive sense (e.g., "I am a speaking animal") but rather as a being that receives the action, the drive, or the address of Being (of existing). It is somewhat like what the French language allows one to say with the verb *vivre* or in German with *leben*: one can "live," without complement, that is be alive, or one can "live an adventure," that is go on an adventure, be carried off on an adventure, experience the contingencies, the risks, and the emotions that it has to offer. On this model, we might attempt to say that "being" in and through an adventure is precisely to live it; and that being this or that, no matter what it happens to be, is not a matter of attributing a predicate to a subject (for example, "I am alive") but rather of living—or practicing or investing or putting into play, mobilizing, taking, gathering or welcoming, inviting, pushing, impelling that which cannot be an attribute without always also being an allure, a coming, an exposition, an excess beyond what would be a pure being-this-thing—which precisely *would not be* but rather would subsist in inertia (not to say in entropy, in a release from what makes it be).

> *The erotic cannot be felt secondhand. As a Black lesbian feminist, I have a particular feeling, knowledge, and understanding for those sisters with whom I have danced hard, played, or even fought. This deep participation has often been the forerunner for joint concerned actions not possible before.*[65]

Ultimately, what's at stake is the desire of the thing, no matter what it is. The desire for the thing and the desire that the thing "is"—which is to say, exposes, advances, and follows. The two desires are the same: nobody comes before the thing in order to desire it and the existence of the thing, whatever it is (the thing in itself), is its own desire. Needless to say, the nonliving—stone, electron, gas, and so on—cannot be considered as a subject of desire: but at stake is precisely the opposite, desire as the thrust whereby it exists.

It: the "thing in itself" in Kant, the "thing itself" in Hegel and Husserl, or in Heidegger. These things are not identical but they all decline pure and simple existing, which, precisely, cannot be pure or simple. It is just as much *Ding* as *Sache*—that is, as much "thingy" as "stuff," "whatever" as well as "intrigue," "process," and "trial." It is both presence in the world, no matter where, no matter when, and presence to the relation-world, relays from thing to thing, little by little and a lot by a lot. The thing, therefore, as the *res*, the real, the nothing according to which all things exist. But what does "according to" mean? Nothing, precisely, nothing but it, which, on the one hand, is plural—there are things, one thing alone would annihilate itself—and which, on the other, arises. What comes in addition to and in place of not one thing.

An excess, an exceedance or transcendence. A thrust of being that has no sense (nor reason, nor cause, nor end) other than to be thrust by . . . its own excess. Which isn't its "own" because there is no property whatsoever that may be attributed to "being."

Short of any property, it happens and it exists. It gives itself because it is not given, it desires itself without being desired by anyone. This is why the thing, the real, remains to be realized. "It lacks something needed for it to be what it is."[66] What it lacks is not some other thing but rather its alterity: the nonthing, the relation or the relay, the coming or the sign, the two together. Two allures of desire whose essence or structure is to desire itself, thus to relay to itself and to annul itself in this relay.

To devour itself?
Yes.
In an ontological devoration?
Yes.
Devoration, absorption, assimilation, intimate penetration of intimacy, the infinite in action, nameless confusion: sex and language as passage to the limit of being. Limit of being: nonbeing, nonsense, power strained in its impotence. Devoration, adoration.

> *While I sodomize her, it seems to me that the whole*
> *sky rips open with the vision of this bestial gesture:*
> *she offers to my savage caress an actual face in her*
> *flesh, and turns her entire soul toward me in the open*
> *lily of her flesh. She plays at gazing at herself in my*
> *eyes with the soft dizziness whose perfect contours she*
> *opens in the light as if into a mouth, and seems to*
> *tempt me by screaming at me to eat her as I devour*
> *myself, to make myself a soul in love with this beau-*
> *tiful fruit, to shove myself through it in greediness for*
> *the earth.*[67]

12

Ass in Air

It will be said that we have gone too far in elevating sex and language to incalculable and ultimately improbable heights . . .

Yes, of course, too far: how could it be otherwise when we are fully within exaggeration? What I have called "carrying off" or "carrying away" cannot go anywhere, cannot be carried off without exaggeration. Assuming, at least, that this is the right term; for, where there is no established measure, it is very difficult to speak of exaggeration. What could be represented by a well measured and framed sex, aligned with rationality? For a long time, we have had forms of measurement linked to demography, political economic, and/or religious programs, projects or tendencies, and many prohibitions of a complex nature. This broad, encompassing control of sexual activity bears witness to the possibilities of disorder that it entails.

But precisely, such possibilities come before all types of order—including those of an animal order that is supposedly "natural" and which, in fact, essentially regulates the estrus, the period of fecundation from which the speaking animal is cut off (except when it is reconstituted by means of calculation). But animal sex remains for us, in some way, sex itself, a vigor and even a violence that we represent as an irruption at the very heart of nature.

> *Ancient animals copulated, even as they ran,*
> *Their glans coated with blood and excrement*[68]

Rimbaud thus composes an agitated, feverish, and exuberant vision of a sex before human beings—and even before animals dominated by humans—excessive, furious, unleashed, projected according to schema of a loss in a world where, from now on . . .

> *no one*
> *Will dare again to raise his genital pride*

—which, of course, sounds like all nostalgia for a never diminished "pride" that desires to regain or to invent for itself an archaic animality—a fantastic animality in the sense that the fantastic, here, does not have the status of a fantasy[69] or imaginary scene, but that of an excess beyond any supposed "natural order" (in the sense in which one commonly says "that's fantastic") and of the transgression of an order within this very order.

Rimbaud's blood and excrement combine with a force that boosts sexual proclivities that are far from being "simply organic"; that highlight or make resonate to what degree sex forms something *aorgic* in the organic realm, to use a word that Hölderlin forged[70] — that is, an element or a register foreign to the organism and to organization, to the pursuit of a design. Freud noted that the upright posture of human beings distances their gaze, their nose, and their mouth from the organs of excretion, which shifts and renders more complex, albeit without abolishing it, the relationship of sex to these excretions. Augustine wrote that "we are born between urine and feces." He adds, very obviously as a subtext: we copulate and conceive in the same way. He does not add, but we should, that we can also enjoy — without conceiving — excretions and their zones.

The aorgic — which we could also call "chaotic" — is characterized by formlessness and lack of intentionality. Excretions drop into the inert or in the maceration of the soup where other organisms come to arise and to sprout. Sperm and the flows that accompany it, the discharge and the liquors stimulated in the vulva, and saliva as well, even tears, are excretions, not waste matter but fluids that are lost as they bathe sexual activity — lost outside or inside, but always beyond the proper and organic body. Menstrual blood should also be added. A multiple and largely generalized liquefaction (like sweat) accompanies what constitutes a passage between organs and thus produces a suspense of the organic, a momentarily aorgic organicity.

The "ancient animals" figure within us, as do all animals, the most archaic of living beings, the chaos of their drives that are useless except to play or impel life anew. No sex without such bestiality, this liquidity, this venting whereby organisms are reorganized, driven by organs that are somehow excessive or supernumerary in comparison to nonsexuated organisms.

Everything thus seems upended, *cul par-dessus tête* ["ass in air"] as one says in French to designate the thorough reversal of the expected order of things. The word *cul* ["ass"] — one of these neither technical nor refined [*châtiés*] (nor castrated [*châtrés*] . . .) words that abound in vulgar languages (in French, often metaphors and metonymies of sex—*"une histoire de cul"*[71] ["dirty stories"]) — is not a simple word; it is a thing, something that cannot be otherwise designated. Nor, in the final analysis, otherwise thought.

The word "sex" itself is situated at the limit. It is an honest word, although rarely devoid of provocative resonances. Its suggestive power is only lost when it is employed for one of the two sexes ordinarily taken for granted, male and female—a difference that we will discuss later. The language of sex only swarms with foul diversities because it must touch on the untouchable, what squats in filth, the dirty, the disgusting, which is also the chaotic, the intermingled, the frenzied, and the panting or the cry. The limit of language or language exhausting itself at its limit — "fuck off!" exclaims the Sadian hero.

Or rather, language in its prolixity, proliferates sexual values in invective or stupefaction—fucking god! whore! cock! bollocks! cunt! motherfucker! fuckhead! dumbass!—as well as in the designation of the act (sometimes called "it") — dancing in the sheets, getting off, knocking boots, shooting a load, *rataconniculer* in Rabelais, making *cattleya* (Swann's coded expression). Deliberately heavy or tacky, contemptuous or cynical, what is called *raw* language traverses all languages, an idiom of derision and the toppling of dignities whose most accomplished form can perhaps be found in Shakespeare:

> *Your daughter and the Moor are now making the beast with two backs.*

This beast with two backs, a fantastic and not so attractive beast, even a little repugnant with the look of a big absurd and writhing insect, replays in clunkier terms the division of what Plato's Aristophanes describes as a halved sphere, their inverted organs seeking to regain one another. In one way or another, the embrace is debased, its force turns into a grotesque jiggling, desire becomes gluttonous avidity, a "job" that appears "flawed and ridiculous," to reprise Montaigne's words. He writes that this act "by its imperious authority . . . makes a brute out of all the theology of Plato and a beast of all his philosophy."[72]

But he adds: "and yet there is no complaint of it." That is to say that Plato does not complain, nor theology nor philosophy. It's not merely pleasure that helps to forget brutishness: it is, on the contrary, the latter that pleases and at its extremity intimates that the irresistible movement that lowers to bestial groaning also transports to sublime beatitude. This is not or not only a dialectic (Hegel admires the fact that the same member can serve both a filthy purpose and a noble purpose) but a passage to the limit in which nothing is negated and then sublated: everything is in the same arousing and ecstatic uplift. In the same excited and berserk fervor.

Until what point? Until the end. Which means?
We are never finished with extremity, the limit,
    passage . . .
To be continued.

13

Penetration

*The sensation was so exquisite that she could have
asked to have it indefinitely prolonged; but suddenly
his head bent lower, and with a deeper thrill she felt
his lips pressed upon that quivering invisible bud,
and then the delicate firm thrust of his tongue, so full
and yet so infinitely subtle, pressing apart those close
petals, and forcing itself in deeper and deeper through
the passage that glowed and seemed to become illumi-
nated as its approach . . .*

    *"Ah—" she gasped, pressing her hands against her
sharp nipples, and flinging her legs apart.*[73]

"I am convinced the most furious material appetites are
formulated *unknowingly* [insciémment] by the élans of ide-
alism in much the same way as the most unclean carnal
extravagances are engendered by the pure desire for the impossible, the ethereal aspiration of sovereign joy. Besides,
I do not know (and nobody knows) what these two words
mean: body and soul, where the one ends, where the other
begins. We feel *forces* and that is all."[74] When Freud was just
three years old, Flaubert already proved him right that artists
are superior in knowledge to psychoanalysts—on the very
subject of what takes shape "unknowingly" [*insciemment*], a
neologism in which gestates the unconscious [*inconscient*]
as well as the nonknowledge that accompanies it in the
philosophers.

    Unknowing [*inscience*] in its own manner says something
that other terms also cover but perhaps do not intimate as
clearly: at stake is actually a sort of knowledge. Flaubert indicates it in single word—"we feel." Feeling consists pre-

cisely in knowing in the sense of having an experience, entering into proximity, familiarity, and even intimacy with something or someone. The paradigm of knowledge is presented most often as the taking cognizance of something, what the Greeks called *mathesis*. Mathematics represents the excellence of knowledge as the construction, the position, and the transmission of a determinate content that can be verified using procedures that are themselves verifiable. This does not mean that mathematical progress and discovery do not operate by research, essays, intuitions, and trials. *Mathesis* itself arises from what Greek calls *gnosis* and that we translate as "cognizance" by way of the Latin *cognosco*, in which the prefix *co-* is joined to *nosco* that connotes an approaching, a becoming familiar, and the having of an experience. It connects the mark of association (which can also suggest intensification) to that of inchoate things (the desinence "sco")—that is, things that are progressive or ingressive, in the midst of beginning.

It would not be surprising if this "cognizance" had in it a bit of the Hebrew *yada*, which designates an active, participatory knowing; and that, in translation, produces the famous "knowing in the Biblical sense," among the first occurrences of which is none other than "Adam and Eve." Elsewhere, "knowing the Lord" can signify sharing his intentions—albeit outside of religious observance, by acts (justice, compassion, etc.)—entering his viewpoint, espousing his intentions. Claudel invented a play on words that consists in writing *connaître* [to know] as *"co-naître"* [co-birth].

Many languages, therefore, make a distinction between knowledge [*savoir*] as consummate possession and knowledge [*connaissance*] as frequentation, proximity, and sharing. Accordingly, *inscience* or nonknowledge must be understood in both registers. There is no content that can be

preserved in a treatise but there is an experience, which
means an advance into the unknown: "we feel forces." We
are thrust. This is also what Freud seeks to underscore by
qualifying the drives as myths. It is a way of speaking an
experience that cannot be transcribed in a language of
knowledge.[75]

The experience—ordeal, practice, usage, exercise—of
such forces takes place between the body and the soul, without their distinction and yet as if by crossing an ungrasp-
able limit. Nothing other than a passage toward an outside
whereby an inside is figured: a passage that distinguishes
body and soul—each, according to Descartes, providing
matter for the other, a compact matter-extension, gathered
in upon itself, and a subtle matter, united at every point to
the body of the speaking animal. The senses have a very
clear knowledge of this union of body and soul; but pure
thought only knows how to distinguish them, such is its
work. The senses know in a very certain and ultimately un-
deniable manner that this union is force expressing itself, in
accord with its nature as force, with its thrust.

Here, in any event, is the best place to grasp the parallel-
ism and intersection of sex and language. For, the latter expresses—presses outside—the ideality of sense as sonorous
materiality, while the former expresses outside the living
being the appetite for life (which it has, which it is).

In both ways, expression is formed by penetration. Language penetrates the thing's obscurity to itself, bringing it to
be signified, that is, transported outside its concrete effective-
ness, repeatable as idea. Sex penetrates the drive's obscurity
to itself, bringing it to enjoy and/or engender (which comes
down to the same thing, as we will see later). Consequently,
language dreams of enjoying and/or engendering the thing
itself ("*fiat lux*") and sex dreams of being transported as idea:
joy, love, ecstasy.

What does she want? To sleep, perchance to dream, to be loved in dreams, approached, touched, almost—almost to enjoy. But not to enjoy: if not, to awaken. But she did enjoy in dreams, once upon a time . . .[76]

Double penetration—of the impenetrable. For, what body or matter mean is impenetrability. The material body is impenetrable but its diverse orifices, each with its own mission and emission, put penetration into play as an idea: the idea of going inside, which does not exist. And what spirit or immatter mean is the impenetrability of what penetrates everywhere. If matter were all there is, we might emphasize, there would be no impenetrability: it would just scatter into pulverized bits and the question of penetration would never arise. This question only ever arises because there is a body, the formation of a contour or a sealed envelope, which immediately supposes—or better, results from—its permeability. Impenetrable is what exposes itself to penetration. Penetrating is what exposes itself to the impenetrable.

Whence hard-ons and fingers, tongues and gazes, things smelled and heard, pressures, scratches, bites, abrasions of the skin; dilations and contractions of all the orifices down to the pores and to the portals of the soul. Penetrate: enter up to the *penus* that is the pantry, the vital reserve. Rape is the negation of sex—and of language. Penetration feeds on life and feeds life—the joy of life because life lives on joy: on the excedence of being.

By now I'd reached her abdomen, massaged it with a rolling circular motion, then descended to her hips, and then, with my eyes on her rosy pubic hairs, I thought of Alice Lee Langman, and Alice Lee Langman's memories of a Polish lover who had enjoyed jamming her cunt with cherries and eating them out one by one.[77]

Extremity of touch, tact of the body rife with orifices and conduits, points of access for holding, withholding, and stroking all along whatever slips in from another body and feels itself held tight, close, bathed, fucked. To touch their being-touched—"the feeling-walls deep in the you-abyss / rejoice, seedpainted one" [*die Fühlwände tief in der Du-Schlucht frohlocken, Samenbemalte*].[78]

The you-abyss is only an abyss because I delve into it: whether it be vagina, mouth, or anus penetrated by member, finger, or tongue, it makes itself felt by both the penetrator and the penetrated, way down to the bottomless bottom whose penetration signifies depth, gathering, comprehension, divination, and mediation.

No penetration without being penetrated yourself. Swallowing the other and being swallowed by them. And here, very exactly, is where penetration happens: where life goes looking in the other for its living nourishment—and/or its death:

> . . . *reaching that warm tuft lapping intoxicating myself clinging to the silky hollow of her thighs I could see her buttocks above me gleaming faintly phosphorescent bluish in the darkness while I drank endlessly feeling that stem growing out of me that tree growing its roots branching inside my belly my loins enveloping me like ivy creeping down my back wrapping around my neck . . .*[79]

14

Too Much, Too Little

It is not any less impenetrable. Penetration itself remains impenetrable. Penetration is the first thing one resists; it is what constitutes the stakes and the game of a necessary resistance, even if reduced to almost nothing, because one knows, in turn, that it will persist in resisting. It will be neither properly "lived" nor properly "known." When it comes to penetration, life and knowledge steal away at their limits. Penetration escapes. One might say of it, in a particularly emphatic manner, what Hegel says of the body in general as the "expression of the inner"—that is, of the "individual" of "being for itself" (relating to itself). This "expression" should be taken literally as the pressing of self outside—that is, as a revelation of self by self. In a general manner, action constitutes the being of the individual and the body is the manifestation of the spirit—that is, not the external apparition of what would otherwise remain inward but rather Being manifesting itself and doing so in such a way that its physical manifestation is—ontologically—its spiritual being.

Now, in a general manner, in action, "the individual on his own no longer retains and possesses himself; rather, he lets the inner move wholly outside of him and he thus abandons it to the other."[80] Hegel presents this manifestation both in the form of language and that of work (also designated as "speech and action"). He then specifies that we can just as well say that these manifestations "express the inner too much as we can say that they express it too little." Double defect, excess and lack conjoined, which, it will have to be grasped, constitute the essence of spirit manifesting itself—in other words, its existence.

If Hegel does not count sex among the acts whereby the individual manifests itself,[81] it is because, for him, sex is the manifestation of the species through the individual (which implies a subordination of pleasure, but I won't linger on this point[82]). But if the manifestation of spirit is envisaged in terms of the effectivity of its existence—each time distinct, individuated, and in constant individuation—sex, language, and transformation would constitute a triad in which general coexistence (the singular plural of speaking beings and through them all beings) occurs in three modes: logexistence, technexistence, sexistence.[83]

Reprising the analysis of "abandonment to the other" as though it was about sex, one could say: this manifestation is *too much* "because the inner self breaks out in these expressions, no opposition remains between them and the inner; they do not only provide an *expression* of the inner, they immediately provide the inner self"; and, at the same time, it is *too little* "because in speech and action the inner makes itself into an other and thereby abandons itself to the mercy of the element of transformation."[84] There are thus two risks: breaking out or alienation. If we leave aside the dialectical perspective that would require deference to the final sublation of the whole of spirit in its comprehensive manifestation, it becomes necessary to remain at the level of the too-much-too-little as the condition of expression—of pressure itself or of the thrust.

Sex obligates us to think the thrust in the origin, as the origin of itself, and at the same time as the infinite *différance* of the origin—and therefore of selfhood. Just as it joins inseparably the individual and the species, the human species and all living things, living things and the universe, in the same way it renders inextricable the excessive force of the thrust and its weakness, its too much and its too little—that is, its pulsation and its coming-and-going. The drive is not a fixed quantity, nor is it measurable (and this is precisely what in denial and anxiety provokes vulgar fantasies of immeasurable sexual prowess, "well-endowed" hunks, "master cocksman," "minxes," "sex-pots"—as well as their opposites, the "dickless" or the "uptight" . . .).

The pulsation of the drive constitutes its life or its being: its spirit or its expression, its spirit as expression, and its expression as, indeed, "breaking open" or "transformation"— each of these terms being inapt to designate what one would expect to be an encounter and an exchange between two clearly identified subjects. Sex breaks open or transforms subjects because it abandons them, because they abandon themselves to it even if this abandonment doesn't proceed with a proper and controlled movement: abandonment entails a faith in what overflows each and everyone because what flows—what pulses—goes through individuals from the species and through the species from the universal penetration of everything through everything, from all spirit through all matter and vice versa.

She twists her black locks while she cums she tresses her hair close to her ear letting come her wetness I push her whispering I gaze the whole time at the lattice of cum slowly fall viscous on the fuzzy corner of the carpet the image of the brain wax in the egg white fibers of the carpet.[85]

Hegel denounces the "immediate given" whereby the inner would lose its propriety. If the immediate is identical to fusion (to pure immanence), it never takes place. It must rather be understood as nonmediation—that is, as the absence of a process of passage to the other and from the other to the same. Sexual confusion is not a process without thereby being an immanence. If there is a process, it only resides in fertilization. Sex as such is infertile: it expresses the pulsation that comes from nowhere and that goes nowhere. Always too much and too little, always transformative and yet foreign to all recognition.[86]

Or rather: lovers mutually recognize themselves as unrecognizable. They recognize themselves as "this interiority that is given to the exterior *as* interior" and that gives to think "that it might seem that interiority as such can never appear on the exterior, it can never be given. . . . A secret, but an essential secret, neither mental nor carnal—the noumenon . . . no longer the having of a secret, whether mental or carnal, but the possibility of the secret; the being of the secret displayed in its exteriority"[87] — in an exteriority exterior to the Hegelian dialectic.

Of course, it's you, it's you passionately, you lost in you or out of you: how to know? It's more and less than you, more and less than me. It's what we accept together one from the other. It's you metamorphosed into an animal, into a plant, a bush, a cloud, a river, etc. In this metamorphosis there is no synthesis, no sublation, no sublimation: Narcissus is a flower which is also Narcissus. Daphne is a laurel bush that is also Daphne. You are you and also this plant or this beast enlaced with me; I am me and also this sap or this claw in you. We are each one to the other, each in themselves and in the other, for oneself and for the other, by oneself and by the other. Neither solitude, nor fusion, or the one like the other: never as alone as when united, confused, indistinctly distinct.

> Is it loving it's not loving but it's just as though one
> still had the gestures of love even without loving I have
> this memory that it's with all the women whom I didn't
> love that will have shared these gestures that one
> should only share with women whom one loves I have
> this memory that I owe to all the women that I haven't
> loved and with whom I shared these gestures that one
> should only share with women one loves that that I
> was alone.[88]

15

Sex Singular Plural

Too much and too little sex, therefore. Too few and too many sexes. There is only one sex, a single "sexual phenomenon," if it can be so named — because it is not certain that it is a phenomenon, that it can appear without also disappearing more profoundly than any exhibition or inhibition would intimate.

Of course, there is only one sex and its very name repeats separation, a word derived from *secare* (to cut) or *sequor* (to follow), which seems more plausible and which entails at once separation, succession, and accompaniment. The same can be said about a noun that evokes generation (as in German or Greek), but then one must resort to other words for the "parts" or "organs" reputed to fulfill the office. On this point, in every possible way, languages are as inherently confusing as they are profuse, as exhibitionistic in their colloquialisms or slang as they are inhibited in their proper usage. Still today in French, despite the general relaxation in linguistic norms, it is not acceptable in every context to use the words *couillon* [dickhead] or *con* [cunt], which are, not by chance, sexual slang terms used as insults.

Sexual insults, so widespread, definitely close to universal across languages, along with sexual jokes, definitely useless across cultures[89] — form the dual testimony of the ex-in-hibition of which sex is at once the subject and the object. This testimony itself presents one facet of what touches, in contexts of sacrality sometimes linked in the same cultures, on other forms of ostentation, ritualization, and/or retention of sexual activity. The amplitude and ambivalence of so many remarkable traits confirms that the singularity of sex makes it unlike any other human behavior. And one should not forget the no less remarkable proliferation of sexual styles, tropes, and manners, as much individual as social and cultural, which multiply along with the regimes of sexualities — of which the LGBTQIA rainbow itself only offers an approximate sense for the real multiplicity of practices and dispositions.

Unquestionably, there are only *idiosexes*, just as there are

only idiolects: speech only exists—and through it language—
in manners, accents, intonations, lexical and syntactical
choices, and mimicry, in each person's pragmatics. And just
as the idiolect itself is never simply one, nor unified, nor
unitary, but rather is diffracted according to circumstances,
registers of expression, and interlocutors, so sex is neither
unique nor unified in any person.

What Pierre Jean Jouve calls *Les Beaux Masques* [The
Beautiful Masks]—unexpected, surprising, morbid, or fre-
netic figures of sex revealed in very honorable people—
never mask anything other than the accepted impulse required by social codes:

> *When in the Bois de Boulogne she spoke to me of the*
> *future and of the lastingness of her love her sad face*
> *had a look of intense warmth; but under her thick*
> *tweed skirt her heavy hips pushed toward me with ob-*
> *scene designs, and I who was afraid of committing to*
> *her too much with words, seeing those hips I loved her:*
> *the day before she had touched her cunt in front of me,*
> *for a long time, in the midst of those hips, and I had*
> *seen her do what she used to as a young girl.*[90]

The important thing is that the codes (such as *tweed*, a
sartorial and linguistic code) are indispensable less to assure
a modesty that would itself be honorable, or even delicate
and courteous, than to dissimulate, more profoundly, the
inexhaustible plurality not merely of "sexual orientations"
but also of tastes and distastes, attractions and repulsions,
haunting ideas, obsessions, games or manias, and better
still, more intimately, more imperceptibly, something that
escapes each person, something that one cannot even sense
and can only be declared out of the blue, or that cannot ever
be declared because there is nothing to declare: how I am
touched, how I touch, if I am touched or touching, alter-

nately or simultaneously, and neither *how* nor *why* matter but merely, barely a *what* confused with a *who* and merely exclamations points or ellipses. . . .[91]

Or rather, like a lover-philosopher writes to his lover:

> *We are Hermaphrodite himself . . . Hermaphrodite, not hermaphrodites despite our bisexualities now un- leashed in the absolute tête-à-tête. Hermaphrodite in person and properly named. Hermes + Aphrodite.*[92]

There is nothing to mask and nothing to unmask. It ex- ceeds any possibility of identification. *It*: enough said. For, if this *it* isn't exactly or exclusively the *id* that Freud evokes to envisage the depths of sex, we are, at least, not far from the anonymity of what remains masked or covered (*verdeckt*) behind the extrusions of the libido, this "original state of things, realized in earliest childhood" still without "object," this "great reservoir" of all ulterior investments that "in es- sentials persists."[93] What persists in masked form and that Freud refuses to dilute in a general psychic energy, what must be recognized to possess a unique sexual character (linked, in addition, to the "special chemistry" of "the sexual processes") can precisely be called "ego-libido" (or "narcis- sistic libido"): this tells us nothing except to teach us that the "ego" is sexual before being sexuated, that sex precedes itself, in sum, as a self-sectioning or self-succession contem- poraneous with the most primitive self-distinction. It is not one sex or the other; it is sex as "ego." Let us not forget that Freud attributed the distinction between the Ego and the Id "not only to primitive man but even to much simpler organ- isms, for it is the inevitable expression of the influence of the external world."[94] Inside/outside, it begins thus.

Even, consequently, before sex? Without a doubt, yes, since we have seen that sex could begin before sex, in can- nibalism or some other form of the metamorphosis of the

inside in relation to its outside (which would mean: exter-
nalization inside before exposure outside).

I = sex. I (s)exes itself, you (s)exes itself, we sexist. An
entire alchemy precedes this highly complex set of relations.
Alchemy, magic, chemistry, processes or maneuvers, recombinations, mutations—whichever. Sex by itself shows to what
extent it indefinitely precedes itself (for where begins—and
where ends—the outside/inside division?) and even to what
extent it succeeds itself. It precedes itself and succeeds itself
in a sexual pluralization that, from then onward, also tends
toward increasing dissociation of generative functions and
sexual agency. The day when it was declared that a lustful
look was already a sin,[95] sex openly assumed the unlimited
breadth that it contained.

> Our sighs replaced language. More tender, more
> numerous, more ardent, they expressed our sensations,
> they marked their progression and the last sigh of all,
> suspended for a time, warned us that we would have to
> offer thanks to Love.[96]

Everyone, however, has a distinct spasm, a voluptuous-
ness or an anxiety, a drunkenness or a distress—nothing indifferent. Not the same jouissance, of course, which varies
along with all of our variations, but a common trait, so common that it is even shared in common with animals (and
with the gods, if one goes by the mythologies from which
our thoughts originate). So common that it is vulgar, so vulgar that it is gross, so gross that it takes us down into the loins,
into the most unfettered and delirious part of the mind, into
the environs of annihilation.

Because this spasm, so singular and so plural, still mul-
tiplies in us—speaking beings—where it is doubled by another division between inside and outside: language puts
I outside, expresses and exposes it by another thrust that

transports it upon another register of ex-istence that could be called in-sistence. "I," a singular model modulated as many times as there are speaking animals, intoned each time in every possible tone up to the infinity of the inexhaustible exhaustion at the edge of which they encounter the fucking other inexhaustible exhaustion.

Behind language, is there another drive? Another chemistry—or alchemy? Or perhaps the same drive, which would divide itself . . . ? In any case, the animal invents itself differently than language does; it attempts to go back toward a before-language whence it would emerge just as sex emerges from an undifferentiated anterior sex. It invents itself as a jaculation, an emission, or a spasm of speech. Tristan gives Isolde her first kiss:

> *Isolde, O Isolde, when theeuponthus I oculise my most inmost Ego most vaguely senses the deprofundity of multimathematical immaterialities whereby in the pancosmic urge the Allimanence of That Which Is Itself exteriorates on this here our plane of disunited solid liquid and gaseous bodies in pearlwhite passion-panting intuitions of reunited Selfhood in the higher dimensional Selflessness.*[97]

16

not a word
I lacked

Such an idiolect must ultimately be lacking, must no longer be spoken.[98] Far too much and far too little, it amounts to nothing. One thus fails. One fails not only to say sex but one can also fail to have it. One can miss one another. One

80 SEXISTENCE

can miss oneself. Oneself or worse: one can miss one's own absence, miss loss, lose the enjoying of loss before having approached it.

It is not merely impotence, anesthesia, frigidity. Nor diversion, distraction, tepidity. Not anxiety, too pompous a word. A faint signal suffices, without even knowing what it is. It subtly deranges. The problem isn't even necessarily that "it's not working." Everything happens as though it was working, but it's still not the right thing. For a certain time (which might be determined quite precisely) cinema abounded with scenes of "afterwards" in which lovers ask each other how it was. Doubt and disquiet about the other, and thus about oneself . . . about sex itself.

The great Peter Bogdanovich film, *The Last Picture Show* (1971), contrasts failed relationships, hastily formed between kids looking to lose their virginity, and a happy relationship in which nothing is looked for but a tenderness is given, without fanfare, almost on the sly. The action is caught up in the economic and social changes rocking a small town, the call of the big city and the shuttering of the only cinema left whose final showing is also a goodbye to an old form of cinema (figured by John Wayne). Farewell to virginity, farewell to a supposedly bygone sexuality, really gone only for a joyless wandering. One year later, Bernardo Bertolucci's *Last Tango in Paris* (1972) seemed to confirm and to reinforce an aimless bitterness at the heart of "sexual liberation," still fresh at that time.

Both films, in any event, constitute quite forceful cinematographic statements. They bespeak a new confidence in cinema, in a renewed attentiveness to a difficult, opaque, or uncertain and yet vibrant reality, traversed and troubled by a desire that gets lost but also definitely finds itself: the desire of cinema must also be discerned in the film, grasped in passing. Both films suggest that sex has a secret truth which its supposed permissive nullification cannot touch, but actually reveals. I won't launch into film analysis here: better to go and watch them again.[99]

Most important is this: sexual liberation brings out into the open as much misery as jubilation, even more actually. Such misery is not new. Sex was never a part of pleasure. Quite simply because desire is incommensurable with pleasure. In truth, we know this, and we have always known it in some fashion. We are in the process of reformulating this knowledge, as has been done many times from culture to culture.

It is no accident that sex has always been a theater of disorders, illnesses, crimes, deviations, betrayals, infamies, as well as comedies, which always unfold upon an ostensibly fictional stage. Shakespeare's beast with two backs appears within a story of the cruel and loathsome exploitation of a purposefully fabricated jealousy. In Dante, the guilt-ridden kiss of adulterous lovers causes the poet wracked with pity to vanish into hell. The wrath of Achilles, the subject of the *Iliad*, flares up when someone steals the prisoner he coveted for himself. Don Quixote's love for Dulcinea, whose name has become synonymous with the lover's blind embellishments, plays a not insignificant role in his madness. To say nothing of Madame Bovary.

Endlessly sex is unveiled as the disillusionment of love, or rather love is unveiled as the bait that lures into sex—whether it serves to propagate the species or to satisfy a coarse appetite. It is always liable to be disappointed, to disappoint itself.

Nonetheless, we know—that is, within us sex knows—that this disappointment is only measured against a fulfillment. Fulfillment is represented as a satisfaction—that is, as a finishing, a completion, a culmination. Now, what defines culmination is overflowing. Desire, by definition, has no pleasure to its measure—which is infinite. But even this, we know. We know that desire cannot be fulfilled, except through excess, and that excess is difficult, perilous, delicate. It seems to lack something: but it lacks nothing. No object. It is always *I* who lack or who lacks myself: and thus *I* is not there, *I* absents itself within its own desire. Because this desire is not its own, does not belong to it. It returns outside. To the outside it must be entrusted. To pleasure, if possible, or else to desire alone—abandoned but recognized.

At bottom, we know this or desire knows it for us. It suffices for desire to trust in itself as desire: broader than any expectation, defying any conclusion, without a last word. Like an outsized illusion and yet certain of not being illusory. All that the fictions of desire and of love show us is that an imaginary that denounces and undercuts itself can also turn into a figure of truth (fiction, figure—same word). Figure—that is, the presentation of a mystery.[100]

However, "broader" can also mean, in accord with the mystery, lighter, flimsier, looser. If sex knows that it knows nothing about itself—except what's most accessible—then it also knows that it never lacks anything. Even when unsatisfied. Satisfaction is not its truth.

Sex is so nothing, Andy Warhol is reputed to have said, although he does not seem to have written it. He did say, "Sex is so abstract," cited at the beginning of Linda Nochlin's preface to a collection of Warhol's photographs entitled *Nudes*.[101] Any noun whatsoever is abstract—man, yellow or straw—when its notion is considered for itself, apart from any relation. And this is not possible except by pushing language outside of syntax because the very definition of a notion demands a linkage between propositions. One thereby tumbles from logic and semantics ("yellow" = the set of characteristics attributable to this term according to the set of possible contexts) into poetry ("a small swath of yellow wall"—in which the word is no longer abstract, but absolute, detached from everything and open to everything). Sex lends itself especially well to this tumble. This is why the important word in each of Warhol's formulas is the "so": so nothing, so abstract . . . so much so that it thereby becomes so concrete, so laden, so communicative . . .

Nonetheless, its poetry soon reins itself in. It slips off the tongue and through the fingers with an irksome noise. It gets excited; it quickly turns indecent, provocative rather than evocative. It falls short of itself; it lacks itself. It lacks in falling short; it lacks in excess. In falling short it is less than sex: it can be a caress, a smile, a song. In excess it is more than sex: it can be a cantata, silence, or a caress once again.

Sex is lacking by the impossibility of being itself. It is not a sexologist. It is not an *Ars erotica*. It is not pornographer. It is not a mystic in ecstasy. It is not a load of cum. It is not this or that. It is all of this and something other. It is also chaste. It is also continent, virginal, and ascetic. It severs itself and succeeds itself.

Now comes another poet:

Sex contains all, bodies, souls,
Meanings, proofs, purities, delicacies, results,
    promulgations,
Songs, commands, health, pride, the maternal
    mystery, the seminal milk,
All hopes, benefactions, bestowals, all the passions,
    loves, beauties, delights of the earth,
All the governments, judges, gods, follow'd persons
    of the earth,
These are contain'd in sex as parts of itself and
    justifications of itself.
Without shame the man I like knows and avows the
    deliciousness of his sex,

*Without shame the woman I like knows and avows
    hers.*[102]

17

Joy

Let us say *joy* in English,[103] at least for the moment, for long
enough to dissipate the problems that adhere to the French
words, *joie* and *jouissance*. The first is overly celestial, the
second overly gluttonous. Let us also forget about *gaudea-
mus*, *gaudrioles* ["hanky-panky"], and *godemichés* ["dildos"].
Nonetheless, it is the same word, the same sense in any case,
a senseless sense, a sense that always makes itself sensed too
much or too little . . .

Let us say joy or *joi* in the language of the *trobar*, the language of the troubadours whose courtly love—which was also
discourteous, it has been said—or *fin'amor* is "fine," refined,
honed, or purified in the extreme only to the extent that it
limits itself to overly or excessively presenting the more, the
plus or the *sobreplus*, as they say—the more than more, or
rather the *sobramar* of an unparalleled, untenable, perilous,
or even anxiogenic pleasure. Insuperable in any event—
as sung by the *trobairitz* Beatriz, the Comtessa de Dia:

> *Handsome friend, charming and kind*
> *when shall I have you in my power?*
> *If only I could lie beside you for an hour*
> *and embrace you lovingly—*
> *know this, that I'd give almost anything*
> *to have you in my husband's place*[104]

What's better than anything, then, is not satisfaction: it is
what holds desire up higher than its pleasure. What has to

exceed pleasure, therefore. Not to disdain it but rather not to remain even a little content with it. Not to take pleasure in pleasure—is it possible? Or rather, on the contrary, is pleasure itself what surpasses itself, what transports itself beyond, what transcends itself and transgresses itself? Isn't this the way in which it enjoys?

The joy of sex is never content: this should be understood to refer to lack as well as excess, to exasperation as well as explosion, to a passage into exasperation outside of itself. Excess is lacking, lack exceeds.

Eros, son of Penia and Poros, the teacher of Diotima, the child of Poverty and Passage. Ingenious, industrious divine child of the lack that foments her demand and of escape artistry, the capacity to pass beyond the calculation of means and ends, having no other end than her own activity.

Joy delights in joy[105]

No other end? What about the child? Precisely, let's speak of him/her! The child could well be that of the species that renews itself through genitors and gestations: but the kissing, the fucking didn't desire a child without *jouissance*. The child is first that of coitus—in which the species delegates itself and even entirely metamorphoses itself into a double fertile animal (and if there is not coitus but rather some other art of insemination, this art, too, is desired by one or two; it is another form of coitus)—and as such, as a child who comes with desire, he/she is a *jouissance*. The child is a joy that becomes autonomous, that bodies itself forth and lives for this joy: in sum, fulfilled joy—which will unfulfill itself for its own benefit. This is precisely why the child is a pleasure in the first place, why one gains enjoyment from a child, plays with him/her, delights in him/her, seeks to hold him/her close for one's own pleasure. Incest is an elementary joy.

She is wearing a jumpsuit, and he, the belt off his
pants, says to her:
   "oh mama, what're you doing, what're you about to
do?" and yet he embraces her,
   Seeming unhappy, almost in tears he keeps talking:
   "oh mama, shit, what're you about to do, mama,"
and he embraces her.
   Then suddenly, embracing the mother in a jump-
suit even tighter,
   "Oh mama, I won't resist," he utters, and she,
holding him tight she too, she responds: "For a long
time now I understood": with these two words, they
crossed the sweet, terrifying frontier.[106]

Like all joy this one threatens to get lost in itself. It must
be allowed to lose itself outside, infinitely. This is the sole
law of sex.

This is also why there is no calculation, no means, no art
of enjoyment. If all art proceeds from the drive, from the
pulsation of desire, the arts are works turned toward others
whereas the flesh is a work is turned toward the inside of
the beast with two backs—an empty inside, an interval, the
space between skin and skin, the rubbing and whacking of
each other at a harrowing rhythm amidst clutching, raging,
and interlocked bodies.

Skyward in air a sudden muffled sound, the
      dalliance of the eagles,
The rushing amorous contact high in space together,
The clinching interlocking claws, a living, fierce,
      gyrating wheel,
Four beating wings, two beaks, a swirling mass
      tight grappling,
In tumbling turning clustering loops, straight
      downward falling,

Till o'er the river pois'd, the twain yet one, a
    moment's lull,
A motionless still balance in the air, then parting,
    talons loosing,
Upward again on slow-firm pinions slanting, their
    separate diverse flight,
She hers, he his, pursuing.[107]

Lull and resumption of flight, renewed uplift that enjoyment carries far from itself and from she and he. Enjoyment gets joy from the other and from itself, gets joy from the other who gets joy from her-/himself who feels her-/himself enjoyed by the other. The one is the joy of the other each for itself each for the other. Even alone.

This thing comes to pass in all directions, it passes from s/he to the other and from s/he to her-/himself, it comes and goes away, at bottom and nowhere. Continuous and discontinuous, confusion of fusion, joyous clarity in the middle of the night and sudden night in the middle of the day. The apparition of disappearance. (Life of a death?)

No need, in any event, for a violent and nocturnal embrace. But where, how, and by what does this dalliance begin? Just as the eagles set off in distinct flights, it arrives in a gaze, in a voice, a gesture, a perfume, a shadow, in a furtive passage. Everything begins anywhere just as any place on the body can become an "erotogenic zone"—that is, not an organ or a function but the indefinite extension of the slightest touch, the least approach.

The woman passerby to whom Baudelaire dedicates his poem keeps the secret of such an inexhaustible passage:

Around me roared the nearby deafening street.
Tall, slim, in mourning, in majestic grief,
A woman passed me, with a splendid hand
Lifting and swinging her festoon and hem;

Nimble and stately, statuesque of leg.
I, shaking like an addict, from her eye,
Black sky, spawner of hurricanes, drank in
Sweetness that fascinates, pleasure that kills.

One lightning flash . . . then night! Sweet fugitive
Whose glance has made me suddenly reborn,
Will we not meet again this side of death?

Far from this place! too late! never perhaps!
Neither one knowing where the other goes,
O you I might have loved, as well you know![108]

What the passerby knows—what everyone knows of these gazes that drink up in passing, that drink passage, legs striding under a dress—is the entire poem, all of its desire and the suspense of its flash. It is the joyous knowledge of a joy all the more alive and all the more acute because it does not deliver or discharge itself in any way: in it, the drive keeps pulsing on.

In his 2015 film, *Right Now, Wrong Then*, Hong Sang-soo recounts two different versions of an encounter between a man and a woman: in the first, the man wants to seduce the woman and she ignores him; in the second, he is lazy, disagreeable, likes to get drunk, and the woman is attracted to him. Almost nothing happens but, after a kiss on the cheek, the girl says "next time on the mouth." There will be no next time; it is too late and yet one can fairly surmise that it was as if they had kissed on the mouth. There exists a sensual and sexual *as if* that is neither a simulation nor an allegory but a tendential, asymptotic truth, wholly given in its arising.

There is no finishing with simulation and simulacra. The ambivalence of Lucretius's simulacra cannot be dissipated: they are appearances of being and yet also beings of appearance. Never so much as in sex are image and body confused.

To see you nude (and even at times to see oneself) is never to see something: it is a blind seeing, an astonishment that strikes the eye. Nudity is a lure and an outrageous truth.

Perhaps we should say that the erotic body, a body in the throes, shaking, rocked with spasms and shivers, wholly becomes its own simulacrum, appears to itself and to the other as a chaos, a falling to pieces, a torment, a convulsion of its own forms, like the simulation of an equally unfigurable glory and abjection. Body becoming spirit and vice versa, confusedly.

Of course, this is also a difficulty, a fear. With joy, everything is to be feared: that it won't take place, that it will take place. That it will take place *too much* or *too little*. That it will slip away or overwhelm. This fear of everything is inscribed in joy as its very nature: as the nature whereby the natural exceeds itself, comes to existence.

Coming to exist is always coming from very far away and going just as far. . . . As Alenka Zupančič writes: "It enjoys, but, as Kant himself says, 'at a distance,' *in solcher Weite*. It enjoys far away from the subject. It enjoys on the side of the Thing (in itself)."[109]

18

Troubles

Athens revealed to me my haughty foe
As I beheld, I reddened, I turned pale.
A tempest raged in my distracted mind.
My eyes no longer saw. I could not speak,
I felt my body freezing, burning; knew
Venus was on me with her dreaded flames,
The fatal torment of a race she loathes.[110]

Desire only arises in trouble: vertigo, whirlwind, derangement—loss. Sex is trouble from its most humble secretions to its most sublime adorations. And trouble it brings precisely because it goes from the most sordid body to the most shimmering soul. It goes all at once, in a single bound and sinuously, by diffusion and confusion. It goes and returns, it enflames each center by the others, one after the other, centers of pleasure and those of suffering. Louise Labé complains:

All of a sudden I laugh & I weep
Taking pleasure in each twinge of pain[111]

If the thrust of life goes forth toward stability, perseverance in being, that of sex instead pulls back, attracts, and withdraws, like hunger. Its thrust is an extraction in an attraction. This is how we should understand Freud's refusal of an undifferentiated psychic energy: the libidinal order is plural, it is *conatus, impetus*, and *tractus*—persistence, impulsion, drive. Before being itself differentiated sex inaugurates a differentiation of its thrust that takes over from the thrust that life introduces into the energy of the *physis*. It waits a moment to take over, of course, but happens quickly enough to form life as an already troubled configuration, a release from continuity. First and foremost, Eros is discontinuity—which is also why it maintains subtle, excellent, and dramatic relations with Thanatos. The desire of lovers to die together does not simply arise from some fantasy of fusion: it is also from an urge to discontinue one another, one in the other, one by the other. (It thus becomes necessary to correct or displace what has been observed about fusion: if the two who desire fusion disappear into it—into its fantasy—it is also perhaps because they desire to die in it, in a suicide that would not be a *sui*-cide but rather a form of sacred murder . . . However, it must be acknowl-

edged that such a sacrifice, which abolishes any distinction
between the sacrificer and the sacrificed, leads into an inextricable confusion . . . One might even add that sacrifice,
where it is practiced—and it never takes place without col-
lective trouble—is clearly inseparable from the social apparatus that frames it and that thereby contains its confusion.
Lovers, for their part, are precisely not a society: they are on
the fringes, on the fuzzy margins.)

Nothing is more troubled than sex or than love, which
is also a name for this trouble: "I loved her and could not,
therefore, see her without that trouble, without the desire for
something more that takes away, in the presence of the one
we love, the sensation of loving."[112] The *more*, once again,
unceasingly the *more* haunts the sexual/amorous domain.
The more and the less, the augmentation of desire and the
diminution of its very sensation.

Sex does not only trouble, it troubles itself, it is trouble
in its essence—which contravenes the very idea of essence.
Indeed, sex is not a substance, nor a subject, nor even a
nature: with it, precisely, nature itself, if such a thing exists,
engages in a play of thrusts that already exceed the thrust of
the living being alone. The Greeks called sex *physis* (qual-
ified by an epithet of gender) but this word itself already
designates a thrust, the outgrowth that forms all growth, the
metamorphosis implied in becoming.

> *. . . the child . . . wild wanderer through the city . . .*
> *harassed by pedophiles on the prowl, youngsters*
> *obsessed with by the threat of rape, a paralyzing fear,*
> *that attraction/repulsion, request to offer up your ass,*
> *obsessive refusal despite having interiorized the knowl-*
> *edge of one's own beauty as a perplexingly feminine*
> *truth . . . found myself once at age five on the ambig-*
> *uously stiff lap of an adolescent hungry for sex, lewdly*

*disguised as a woman in gauzy intimate apparel, on
the sly during the siesta.*[113]

Sex is the name for an elementary trouble, a trouble
that besets the self-equality that underlies, in principle, the
element—the part or the simple milieu. Sex is anything but
simple, in every sense that it must be understood. And it
must be avowed: nothing about sex has been understood,
even with mastery over all the phenomena of the division
and the recombination of gametes and also those of the attraction and the conjugation of all genders. If sex were ever
to be considered as an element, it would be the element
of trouble—which is why Judith Butler's formula, *Gender
Trouble*, says something else than its translation into French
as *troubles dans le genre* ["gender in trouble"]: it might also
say (independently of any commentary or discussion of her
own explanations) that gender is troubled not only because
the stability of sex and gender assignments today has been
shaken but also because this shaking bears witness to a
trouble inherent to sex—to non-"gendered" sex, one might
dare say.

Such a sex does not exist, of course, no more than a non-
sexuated sex, a nonliving living being or a nonbeing being.
But precisely, each of these terms indicates an extremity of
signification that signals a passage to the limit: a being is
a being but what its "being" signifies does not pertain to
beingness or beinghood [*de l'étance* or *de l'étantité*]. The
life of a living being, perhaps, does not pertain to language.
Or not to language as an instrument of categorization, nor,
for that matter, as an agent of performance. It could even
be said that everywhere in language reigns a general—and
constitutive—trouble of signification. But there are nodal or
crucial points, points at which signification cannot be sus-
tained beyond the instant that suffices to perturb it (which

might be its constant condition, if it gave up on itself . . .). This trouble is that of sense, which affects itself with its own escape: it thereby affects itself, senses itself—and knows itself—not culminating in an ultimate or supreme sense. This sensing surfaces in language and as language: speaking animals feel—and thus know (by what "knowledge?")—that they don't have access to their own sense or to the sense of "being" and of "life" in general.

There is nothing less in sex than an opening of such a trouble of sense. Sex is not simply a matter of biological differentiation but also, at the very least in the speaking animal, a perturbation of biology that arises from and within the biological order itself. Sexualities are neither simple nor even, ultimately, clearly identifiable. As we have already said, even the reproduction of the species is opened or exposed, in human beings, to new techniques, institutions, and affects. About the deeply enigmatic and ambivalent enjoyment that precedes and exceeds reproduction, it suffices to posit this question: why, in order to speak of "the absoluteness of the absolute" or the "gathering in which being comes together with itself," should a philosopher, to such an end, borrow the term "feeling" [*sentiment*] from Pascal? What should this philosopher resort to the sexual lexicon of jouissance, of *joie-et-souffrance* [joy-and-suffering], of modesty and gentleness?[114]

Why? if not because, even where "words fail," the trouble caused by this failure babbles in words for sex: in them can be heard something other than sense. In them sense feels itself to be troubled. Amphibology is consubstantial with it. "For every manifestation of bare sexual life the seal of its recognition remains the insight into the equivocalness of its nature. This is also confirmed in virginity. About all, the ambiguity of its intactness is evident."[115]

Perhaps the equivocation begins with this, that the drive

pushes in two directions at once—both of them infinite: on the one hand, reproduction, making babies, and on the other hand, joy, making love. Two types of "making" share conjunction and disjunction in the same space, the same indeterminate zone.[116] At the same time, this sharing is that of a tension and a pleasure, whose essential rhythm gives measure: the coming-and-going of the caress that keeps giving the erogenous zone back to itself, to its indetermination, up to the point when it has to stop. But it never stops and any supposed endpoint (discharge, ecstasy, exclamation, expir . . .) would not suppress the equivocation.

> *You should have seen her after those sleeping bouts, still swollen, her organs exultant, ecstatic under her rosy skin. At such times she was funny, as laughable as other people. For some minutes she'd reel with happiness, then the full light of day would come to her and delivered, as if too heavy a cloud had just passed, she'd resume her glorious flight . . .*
>
> *All that can be fucked. It's extremely pleasant to grasp this moment when matter becomes life. You rise up to the endless plateau that spreads out before men. "Whew!" you go. And again "Whew!" You come the limit up there, and then it's like an enormous desert . . .[117]*

With the equivocation, what remains is an unsharable sharing, a division of sex in itself by itself. Into "genders," if one wishes, but in the gender of allure, facet, touch. Masculine and feminine, of course, but without forgetting that each side is only the section of a whole that does not exist (that exists as a fleeting individual, not as a unitary species or as a unitary gender). The One is the fiction that the section will have always already come first. Consequently, each sectioned segment envelops its share of the One—or more exactly, since it is a fiction, each segment envelops the One. Each time it is the One taken into a — real — segment of its — fictive — unity. There is nothing surprising in the fact that the masculine and the feminine can, in each case, envelop one another, develop one another, mix and unmix with one another.

One might attempt to distinguish them as "man" and "woman" — allowing for all the familiar reservations about such distinctions since Tiresias[118] — but this only opens the inexhaustible series of interpretations of these two terms. They can be understood successively as the continuous and the discontinuous (or if one wishes, *she the continuous* or *he the discontinuous* — or the reverse), or as nature and culture (the traditional couple, the one that Kant, for example, inverts), or as discharge and surcharge (to play with the relatively common, and Freudian, model of jouissance as "discharge"), or, with Lacan, known jouissance and unbeknownst jouissance [*jouissance sue et jouissance insue*] (jouissance of the phallus or jouissance of the body[119]): in every way, all of these attempts to understand, none of them vain and none conclusive, require that we return to a division that is unnamable because it is intrinsically trouble and troubled.

Perhaps it is the difference signaled above, between a feminine being-in-the-world and a masculine being-in-the-world. But this would mean that the "world" — that is the space open to a circulation of sense — is itself the opening to what exceeds it, comes to it from elsewhere or exposes it to an outside: its sense, the sense that it is, not that which it would be supposed to "have." The polarity of sexual accents and the plurality of their declensions in all genders is analogous to that which pulls language between syntax and semantics: each one the other's outside and its possibility — with all the declensions in all languages.

This difference or this *différance* does not divide a unity
and does not envision one. In a sense it does not divide or
envision anything; it divides an already-divided that redi-
vides and shares itself out indefinitely in every case—and
every case, here as elsewhere, every fall, occurrence, and
occasion never have anything in common, anything except
"sex" or "language"—along with the trouble they bring.
Nothing but trouble, each time banal and singular, an emotion as proper to each and everyone as every emotion but
whose resonances, intonations and ways of happening are
as varied as all the allures, the zones, and the vibrations of
all the registers of a body that entirely becomes a physiognomy, an expressivity, an idiosyncratic nature, an idiosex
that speaks an idiolect. Each and everyone makes love like
no one else—even though everyone basically does it alike.

Michèle Gennart:

> From the other sex we don't only expect they will com-
> plete us by adding to us a part that we lack [. . .]
> We get enjoyment from the fact that, desiring their
> other, the other sex invokes and provokes our own
> sexual determination and thereby makes our own part
> itself something perfect.[120]

Benoît Goetz:

> If there is a history of sexuality, there is a geography of
> the sexes, in the sense that we elaborate here. The sex-
> ual vessel [bateau sexuel] (Lacan) and amorous des-
> tinerrance (Derrida) cross oceans and accost territories
> that artists and writers have already explored. Neither
> masculine nor feminine, a sex is a "struction," a mass
> of images, ideas, manner, and thoughts that stratify its
> territory. A singular tangle of pleasures, desires, pain
> and enjoyment.[121]

E. E. Cummings:

I like my body when it is with your
body. It is so quite a new thing.
Muscles better and nerves more.
i like your body—i like what it does.
i like its hows.[122]

If there is an enigma of jouissance, it is because there is a jouissance of the enigma whose name designates a speech that is extraordinarily meaningful. Like that of the Sphinx or the Sphinge who herself, undoubtedly, is nothing other than the double enigma of sex and language.

And during this time I spoke with her, and she with
me. And I felt like a wise man, I had the impression
of understanding everything, in the single indistin-
guishable flame of the masculine and the feminine.
We uncoupled and coupled anew, at another point of
our bodies and of the world. I penetrated even further,
to a point that no man and no animal had been able
to reach. We gazed at one another and contemplated
the single root of our two adjoined bodies, with its
pornographic and cosmic light. Then we fell silent
and spoke only with sexual gestures in the fiery sea of
contemplation.[123]

19

Love Unto Death

Love battles for life and for death.[124]

Why joy? Why joy together with jouissance or else without it? Why jouissance also without joy? Why joy as the augur of a passage to the limit? But which limit? Precisely that limit which might place joy and jouissance in continuity or discontinuity.

A limit that is imperceptible, unlocatable, essentially labile and fleeting. And yet clear enough that, most of the time at least, it is unmistakable. We know very well, in fact, with a knowledge of the world and not of consciousness—to speak like Merleau-Ponty—or rather with a knowledge in us that is the world's rather than our own, how repletion, fulfillment, and satisfaction coincide with seizure, commotion, and alarm. We know in what way the violent jolt of the thrust is suspended between crisis and fervor. How, otherwise, would rape be possible? As if it wasn't also an outrage against oneself, the pillaging of one's own jouissance . . . Rape is only possible in the negation not only of the other but also of sex itself. It only affirms it by negating it. It supposes the violent exigency of such negation.

But isn't such negation inscribed within sex? Isn't it the very thing that exists or makes exist outside of itself, outside of continuity even as it assures and seeks and demands a continuity that can only come to it in the coming of an other—the child, this stranger who goes on to exist for itself—or rather, in the confusion that never ceases to graze, to dream, and even to attempt fusion: that is, death?

This is why rape can be mimed, simulated but truly and lovingly approached—all along an *infrathin* limit . . .

Let us return to Bataille: "erotism, the approbation of life right up to death." *Right up to*: this is the limit because there is no "inside" of death. What is approved is the limit, precisely. This approbation is comic and tragic at the same time.[125]

It is comic because what it approves is nothing; it escapes upon being affirmed, slips away in a spasm. As one knows, sexual comedy is inexhaustible, from the bawdy lexicon to innuendos, from erotic tales to farces. And what is it one laughs at? At a mistake, a doubletake, the unforeseen upsurge of the obscene, of the dirty, of the lowly—of the ass-backward. And thus always of an inversion or resolution into nothing, into derision. Saying, as she displays her sex, "I am God," Bataille's Edwarda is as comic as she is terrible, as laughable as she is vertiginous. What laughter approves is always a capsizing.

This capsizing of the same is also what tragic bitterness approves, neither with sadness nor desolation nor drama but the acute knowledge that a truth arises in a loss. Better: that the truth always arises in its loss. This is the other face of comedy: one does not capsize into nothing; and it is the truth of relation, of life, and of sense. The two faces are inseparable; but their association is what gives rise to desire, the thrust, the drive for itself.

In a quite strange erotic sonnet—involuntarily comic and tragic, rather grotesque, cruel, and disturbing—Fredrich Schlegel writes:

Und wenn du schreist, so schlitz' ich deinen runden
Und weichen Leib mir auf mit kaltem Streiche.
Dann saugen sich die Lippen deiner Wunden
Um meinen Schwanz, daß ich vor Lust erbleiche.
Jedoch, mein Glück, es reift nicht aus zu Stunden:
Du riechst schon sehr, mein Torsoschatz, nach Leiche.

And when you scream with a cold blow
I slit open your round and white body
Then the lips of your wounds suck
At my cock that I blanch with pleasure
And yet, my luck, it doesn't ripen in hours:
Now, my darling torso, you smell strongly of a
     corpse.[126]

There is something unbearable in this poem, the immediate putrefaction of enjoyment that must be considered for
a moment—but that is no less a lie than the exaltation of a
sublime embrace—described, for example, in a letter from
Alfred de Musset to George Sand:

> *Do you know what it means for a heart clenched so*
> *tight that it almost stops beating to dilate for a mo-*
> *ment, to open up again like a poor, dying flower and*
> *to taste once again a drop of vivifying dew?*[127]

We are far from such Romantic hyperboles. But they are
still indicative of something—after other, Baroque or mystical hyperboles, and before the crude and cruel hyperboles
of our time—those of Bataille, for instance:

> *Your breasts open like a coffin*
> *and laugh at me from the beyond*
> *your two long delirious thighs*
> *your stomach is bare like a death rattle.*[128]

What erotic and amorous hyperbole indicates, with its
very hyperbole, with its excess and its breathlessness, with
its fierce exhaustion in emphasis, is a knowledge that wants
to be said but cannot be.

Or rather, a knowledge that does not want to be said
because it knows that it must be. It knows that it must be
fulfilled in what is called a sacrifice: the actualization of
a relation with the impossible (the outside of the world).
The proximity, not to say the conjunction, in Bataille, of
erotism and sacrifice is a function of their profound sacri-
ficial cohesion. Both are a form of "comedy" because each
one renounces any access to actual death—here, one lover
with the other, and there, the sacrificer with their victim.
Sex, in fact, is closer to the truth of sacrifice than is ritual sacrifice; and this is why, in Sade, there appears more
clearly than elsewhere the demand for death at the hands

of an executioner—whose avoidance signals that the farce is complete.

He who enjoys by hanging himself and arranging for someone to cut the rope at the moment of orgasm is the pinnacle of comedy. Comedy revolves around bloodshed. But it sidesteps cruelty (*cruor* is the Latin word for spilled blood). Sex is raw—and it thereby revolves around cruelty or crudity and menstrual blood and blood that might spurt with the exasperation of irritated flesh, biting, squeezing, and abrading. Many sexual practices flirt with torture, which, in turn, often lets appear its jouissance.[129]

Raw sex touches on its own limit: the unlimitedness of bloodshed, cruelty that without any doubt arises from its very thrust, from life that approves itself through death.

20

Love Unto Life

His trembling hands went out to her,
Her cool flesh made his senses blur;
While, head thrown backward, sinking dim,
She opened wide her soul to him . . .
Past his life went whirls of lights,
Chaos of music, days and nights,
Her wild eyes yearned to lure him in
And close him up in dark of sin,
To lure him in and drink him down
And all his soul in love to drown. . . .
Her nakedness he seemed to see.
And breast to breast, and knee to knee,
Tremulous, breathless, swaying, burning,
Body to beautiful body yearning,
In joy and terror, flesh to flesh,

They flamed in passion's fine red mesh,—
Living in one short breath again
The cosmic tide's whole bliss and pain,
Darkness and ether, nebulous fire,
Vast suns whirled forth by vast desire,
Huge moons flung out with monstrous mirth
And stars in glorious hells of birth,
All jubilating, blazing, reeling,
An orgiastic splendor wheeling,
Moon torn from earth and star from sun
In screaming pain, titanic fun,
And stars whirled back to sun again
To be consumed in flaming pain! . . .
In them at last all life was met.[130]

Sex itself, if it does not really die and if it remains at-
tached to the entire course of existence, at the very least
grows and diminishes. It arises, it rises up and takes off in
a long pulsation. It begins and it continues in tenderness,
passing through jolts, vertigo, and fright. It continues dis-
continuously. It allows for its interruption, the strange clarity
that separates its nights, the distinction that gives rhythm to
its confusion, a scansion in which the caress by itself spaces
itself out, suspends itself and awaits itself.

This means that sex understands itself both as raw and
as . . . The evil genius will say "cooked." It's cooked, it's
fucked, it's the family and sexual moroseness. But it's not
so simple. The family isn't so simple: it decomposes itself,
recomposes itself, displaces itself, transforms itself with the
transformations of sexual practices. Cooking can be a matter
of art, a know-how that also knows how to make love.

Not that it doesn't remain raw and rare, perhaps. Because
it is always a matter of this, that fusion knows itself to be
fictive because it is incompatible with division—with sex it-

self. The amusing scene in which Hephaestus offers to weld two lovers together in his forge is as desirable as it is vain. The lovers who hasten to consent know that they will lose whatever joy they stand to gain. What they consent to in it is the hope for compensation beyond this world. The lovers have a knowledge about their encounter: it is an encounter, precisely. In an encounter, there is arising, irruption, strangeness, and opposition as much as proximity and contact. The lovers, the lips, the sexes each come up against one another.

We know something about this conjunction of grasping and letting go, contraction and abandonment, opening and closing, being transported and being transfixed—and the one and the other, and the one in two, and the two in a confused melee, the knot and the unknotting, destitution and denuding. We know how much we don't know, how extreme is our inability to know anything about what we attain—and what attains us.

This nonknowledge is comedy as much as tragedy: irrepressible laughter and astounded stupor in the face of the truth, which is not the truth of disjunction, but the truth itself disjointed, confused truth. Isn't it for this reason that Plato's *Symposium* comes to such a surprising end, recalling the discussion struck up after the discourses on love? Socrates explained to Agathon and Aristophanes that comedy and tragedy pertain to the same art and the same artist. Agathon is a tragic author, Aristophanes a comic author. But each of them only agrees inadvertently, as they sink into sleep. And the one who recounts this epilogue, Aristodemus, confesses that he too was falling asleep and couldn't remember the lesson very well. Socrates, as usual, goes to the shrine of Apollo Lyceus. The philosopher carries with him the knowledge of an encounter in which tragedy and comedy remained confused. As always, philosophical knowledge essentially

withdraws. But in withdrawing it makes the truth appear—
albeit divided and confused in its clarity. Accordingly, the
three characters involved in this epilogue were the only ones
really to speak of Eros for itself.[131]

We cannot know what we actually know—less about
sex than in it and through it. For, we have been caught,
touched, jostled, and pushed. We cannot not be—in every
possible way, not excluding refusal, repression, or avoidance,
as well as artistic or spiritual sublimation: for, these terms
all designate the indefinite extensions, the subtle or surrep-
titious arborescences of a passage to the limit, of which the
division of sex forms both the agent and the place.

How does this sharing at the limit happen, this sharing
of a limit that separates while clasping, that joins while
disjoining—disjoining each one with itself and the couple
with its very copulation—come along with such an ample
and ancient cohort of figures of complementary contrari-
ness, indifferent difference or consenting resistance? Yin
and yang, heavens and earth, substance and dissolution, positive and negative, male and female . . . what is at stake in
these oppositions except this, that difference in general only
matters if it isn't posited but is allowed to play itself out: to
play out its contrast, its traction, its attraction, its retraction
and contraction—even its distraction (it veers away and then
back into the game)?

This comic and tragic play is that of the drive, of its own
division between tension and pause or the defusion toward
which it tends: the division of sex is as much the division
between sexual poles and between desire and pleasure,
rising and falling, continuity and discontinuity—life and
death. Without entering into the extensive debates around
Eros and Thanatos undertaken by Freud, Lacan, Derrida,
Lacoue-Labarthe, and Baas—among others—I content myself with this: death is a form of enjoyment, enjoyment a
form of death. Almost nothing separates them, the thinnest

of lines, like that which cleaves each sex and thus makes it what it is: an opening to the other. To the other insofar as he or she is on the other side—the side of otherness of which nothing is appropriable or assimilable, even if the division of the two endlessly traverses each supposed sexual identity.

Death: there where an existence comes to a close, an opening. There where it comes to a close by its own movement, a return upon itself of the open. What we call "love" tarries exactly upon the edge of this return. Love: to desire one another completely open, which means also completely closed. Desire itself—which desires nothing but that, being-to-the-other as being-to-self. Not to be oneself except in an irreducible encounter with the other—and, why not, unto death. Death unto life.

> And what if there were, sometimes, cruelty in not putting to death? And what if there were love in wanting to give death by twos, one to the other, one for the other, simultaneously or not?[132]

The drive knows itself and behaves as this double relation: to the other/to self. It knows that its thrust, and the arising of desire, pushes to this: not to subsist, to exist, to sexist. Whence comes privative love that wishes to exempt itself from separation, to possess the other right up to death, as well as its reverse, oblative love, that wants the other for their own existence, in order to abandon oneself to them. This is what, in one sense, we call *love*, a sense that undoubtedly comes to gather without unifying all the senses of this prolific, exuberant, senseless word: desire, concupiscence, delection, inclination, adoration, abandonment, possession . . .

> . . . the craving
> endless, each one
> beneath you, above you

know, each one that
is dark, nothing bright
at all, the flesh being
bright enough[133]

Love is aroused by sex just as sex is excited by love. What love wants to tender between giving and taking, sex tenders between abandonment and embrace. The one is the truth or the virtue of the other. But each one can also turn away from or bypass the other, because they can each occupy one pole or other—life, death, ex-istence or in-sistence.

There where sex keeps silent or else proclaims "I enjoy," love keeps silent or proclaims "I love." Language in each case passes to its limit and designates "the sovereign moment at which it no longer holds good" (Bataille). But it is not the same sovereign moment in each case. It is almost the same—and one could go as far as hearing the one in the other or the one as the other, especially because in each case one has no idea what one is saying. One is at the extreme edge of sense. There is only a difference of address. An incalculable and undoubtedly unreachable difference—one cannot separate sex from love even in their most incompatible forms—a difference itself always in displacement between the unstable terms.

If, nonetheless, it is correct that when I say, "I enjoy," I appropriate something—a thing that might be unnamable and undecidable—and when I say, "I love you"—a "you" that could very well be myself, in the final analysis—my only consideration is the otherness of the other (itself unnamable and undecidable), then we should say with Pasolini:

> *But, I repeat, true intercourse—as possession was the*
> *possession of something fatally limited. By definition,*
> *in fact, one cannot possess the whole.*
>
> *Rather, being possessed is an experience cosmically*
> *opposite to that of possession. . . .*

On the other hand, it is beyond dispute that the
Possessor is an Evil, in fact is, by definition, THE Evil;
therefore, being possessed is what is farthest from Evil
or, rather, is the only possible experience of the Good,
as Grace, life in its pure, cosmic state.[134]

The inversion of possession into being-possessed can also
be said otherwise: in Spinoza, the dependency of a passion
upon an "external cause" gives an "inadequate idea" because
it supposes a correspondence with something other than itself (with an object). If, on the contrary, affect is detached
from the thought of an object and is entirely joined to the
"adequate idea" of its own power or virtue, it is no longer,
we might say, a pathological affect but rather a logical one.
Accordingly, "the result will be that not only are love, hatred,
etc. destroyed but also that the appetites or desires that are
wont to arise from such an emotion cannot be excessive."[135]
Freely extrapolating, I suggest that the idea of the "object"
or the "external cause" are equivalent, in Pasolini, to that of
"possession" that is actually a form of dependency, since it
is "being possessed by Something limited." Consequently,
the release from dependency on the "object" says the same
thing as Pasolini's "being possessed": desire that is open to
itself as to the desire of nothing, nothing but everything in
God—that is, just as well, in Nature, or in Pasolini's "cos-
mos." Being possessed is being.

Desire, then, "cannot be excessive," which can be understood in two ways at odds with one another but not contradictory: desire moderates itself by itself—otherwise, no
matter its strength, as a force of nature, it could never be
excessive. At the same time, we necessarily come to understand that existing can only be coexisting: traction, contraction, distraction, retraction . . .

Nonetheless, there remains a tension without which
there would be no pulse. Desire could never wholly moder-

ate itself nor ever be confused with a tranquil force of being. Spinoza's *conatus* seems suspended between the perpetuation of an already elevated speed and the impetuousness of an élan. Paul Audi writes: "The whole beauty of desire lies in the imminence of love."[136] He is perfectly correct. But it must be decided how we modulate the sentence: should we emphasize *imminence* or rather *love*? Or is it that love is always imminent, and therefore desiring, but thus always elusive?

21

Erotic Novel

Sex tends hardly to speak itself, language tends hardly to speak it. Pudeur belongs to *eros*; and *pornography* (the prostituted graphism, text, or image) consists precisely in showing what hides away.[137] This is also what pudeur suggests, even what it riles up or arouses through its withdrawal: the only difference is that it suggests through delicacy and even refinement. The word *pudeur* bears a certain relation to *stupor*, the seizure in front of a limit and its increasingly inevitable transgression. For, at the same time, this inevitability knows itself as impossible—more exactly, as nonpossible in the sense we have already examined.

To say or show stupor, a form of commotion made of fright, trouble, and torment—desire tormenting itself, exceeding itself in accord with its most intimate movement—comes down to saying or showing the *inter-dict*: what falls between words, there where showing is no longer possible, if all showing consists of a "here it is!"

For, the "here it is!" is exhausted in its gesture—and its gesture, thereby, in order to be solely the gesture that it wants to be, exacerbates itself. Accordingly, the visual gesture, which draws, paints, photographs, or films, is often threatened with being exhausted in its showing, with showing itself metamorphosed into erection or squirting, into sweat or drool, and indeed into a bulging gaze.

In order to be erotic, visual art must defy vision. Allied with vision, it becomes either voyeuristic or exhibitionistic — that is, it becomes a sexual behavior itself—unless it wishes to show something other than an unexposable sex: a symbolic, a sentimental evocation or even an entire apparatus concerned with the relation of sex to the invisible, to what is too visible or not visible enough. A good example is Marcel Duchamp's very famous *Étant donnés*, which can only be viewed through a hole in a door. What it lets be seen, makes seen, or obliges one to regard—with regard to sex—is commented on or phrased by Jean-François Lyotard in this way:

> *The vulva that you can't fail to notice—it's all you*
> *see—is denuded of all hair (whereas the armpits are*
> *hairy—this isn't a child); the thighs are pried apart*
> [écartelés]; *the erect large labia are open. They let us*
> *see not only the tumescent small labia but also the*
> *gaping orifice of the vagina and even the swollen ves-*
> *tibulary bulbs around the lower commissure. The vulva*
> *elevates sight? Or the vulva-full raises sight?* [La vulve
> élève la vue? Ou la vulvée léve la vue.][138]

To raise sight: certainly not to elevate it, because there is a difference; it is thus akin to "raising one's gorge," today a somewhat rarified phrase to express disgust, repulsion. *Sex raises sight*: it revolts sight.

The philosopher, then, minutely describes with cold anatomy—which also happens to accentuate the traits of the work in question: for example, the word *écartelés* ["pried apart"], a torture word invited but not required by the spreading of thighs wide apart.

Of sex too much or too little is shown. This remains the case if one makes sex into a musical or choreographic theme: although in manifestly different ways, it is possible to say that each confronts us with the question of anatomy in a broad sense: bodies in the act of desire, the caress, the embrace, their aspects, their motions, their sounds or their noises, their scents or their odors, their textures, their sweat, their contractions. Dance and music might make reference or allusion to such things, but their evocation, their insinuation, their recall constitute a detour, employing one form of mediation or another whereby sex remains, precisely, evoked: called from afar, entreated to come be done or be felt without thereby being presented. Nothing perhaps more than sex provides an occasion for allusion or evocation, for undertones and overtones, for the inaudible, the unheard of and the hint, for the well-nigh, for offering up to substitution, slippage—and thus also for joking, banter, and licentiousness . . .

Music gives the entire measure of the gap between sexual evocation—all music being capable in one manner or another of pulsing and resonating with appeal, expectation, and attraction—and sexual sonority: without a doubt, the only musical piece that presents itself as manifestly erotic music (and not as added ambiance . . .) is Erwin Schulhoff's *Sonata erotica*, composed in 1919 for solo female voice. It does not evoke but much rather transcribes or reproduces the groans and heavy breathing of a real act. Not far from pornography even if this wasn't the composer's intention.

Sex withdraws from art because it withdraws from form. If it retains the very energy of the creation of forms, it is formless on its own; or rather, it deforms all forms, beginning with those of the bodies that it puts into play. It has been said: sex indistinguishes forms; it turns away from their exposition. Instead, it commits them, turns their skin out [*les expeause*]: skin touches skin and their forms vanish into zones. The zones exist according to the gestures that agitate them, move them, run through them, and displace them. Form implies a relative autonomy whereby it fulfills itself for itself—a curve, a tint, an arpeggio. Zones appear and disappear, come up and go away with an act or a series of acts that are all strained, impelled, and carried by what exceeds them and is no longer either an act or a state.[139] "Obscenity gives a moment of flood to the delirium of the senses," writes Bataille.[140] Sometimes, art can open the floodgates:

> *I like to see my own sex, I like its form, its color, its smell. Much has been said about the form of the vulva. All sorts of comparisons and metaphors have been tried. All I know is that it pleases me. Enormously.*
>
> *I often place a mirror between my thighs. Or I contemplate myself standing up, my legs spread apart, in the bathroom.*[141]

Sex has an irreducible and intractable *actuality*—more than an activity: either it's sex or not sex, there is no in-between (which, nonetheless, does not contradict the fact that it can be initiated by the imperceptible actuality of a furtive gaze). It is an actuality—a full, effective presence— entirely turned into itself: the actuality of the thrust, its essential overflow, that of a penetration that penetrates nothing but itself, which develops itself and envelops itself in its own skin, which spreads and spills itself out as its own flux.

> *There was the apparition of this girl of stunning grace at a gathering of academics out on the town. There was my tipsy mind that night, there was the sea salt on our skin, there was my sex in hers, our insatiable*

> *mouths, her legs knotted almost outlining a lotus*
> *flower, there was the rain one day on our hair, her*
> *lashes, the rain dotting the sand where we lay inter-*
> *laced, there as the blue glow of the large noctilucent*
> *jellyfish around our final dinner, the Mexican sky, the*
> *dogs wandering along the water's edge, the garbage*
> *fires in the night, and then none of this that was*
> *beautiful, there to be enjoyed, like pure events, without*
> *question, no longer was, her small copper breasts, her*
> *laugh, her cello voice, the trembling of my hands when*
> *I saw her, when they got close to her skin.*[142]

The actuality of sex is at the same time only its own possibility, or more exactly its own thrust, the élan that carries it
toward its own beyond of the possible and of the impossible.
Toward a more-being than being . . .[143] that is *its own sense* in
an absolutely sensible manner and that, in the speaking animal, is confined to language more than to anything else—all
the more so, undoubtedly, if language forms precisely the
distinctive trait of this animal, along with the traits that "hu-
manize" its sexuality, as we have recalled, which are precisely
the traits of both the distancing *and* intensification of sex.

One of these traits appears in the form of the desire to say
what passes to the limit of sense.[144] Saying sex is like saying
language itself: it makes sense where it is experienced. It is a
silence or an embrace. It is an exclamation—in the most rig-
orous sense of the word. Desire salutes itself, less as the desire for sense than as desiring. As Marguerite Duras affirms,
one says "I love you" not to someone but rather to love.[145]

This statement can be modulated to become: one says
"I love you" to love *as someone.* Indeed, one says "my love."
And without the slightest doubt love exists nowhere but each
time, if only for a single instant, in a presence or a touch.

Love implies dependence—not only in its pleasure but
by its very existence and in what precedes its existence:
in our very desire to exist—dependence on half a
hundred odd little things: on two lips (and the smile
or grimace they make), on a shoulder (and the special
way it has of rising and falling), on two eyes (and their
expression, a little more flirtatious or forbidding), or,
when you come down to it, on the whole foreign body,
with the mind and soul enclosed therein—a body
which is capable at any moment of becoming more
dazzling than the sun, more freezing than a tract of
snowy waste.[146]

Writing thus, Jean Paulhan already comes close to narrative and imagistic writing—at the moment when he introduces the reader to a fiction that is not only an imaginary
story but the recitation or declaration of a representation of
love, of a fantasy or, if you prefer, of an allegory, but also of
a not unlikely adventure that opens with two possible versions of the beginning and closes with the suggestion of two
possible versions of the end. Fiction does not merely consist
in the invented character of a story: invention is only the
external face of a speech that cuts its own path toward an
extremity where it will designate itself as exceeded.

Bataille concludes *Erotism* by evoking an objection that
Jean Wahl made to him: "Consciousness of continuity is no
longer continuity, but there is no more speech for all that."
And he pursues: "Jean Wahl had taken my meaning exactly.
I answered him straight off and told him that he was right,
but that sometimes on the borderline continuity and consciousness draw very close together."[147]

It is this closeness that I designate here as "fiction": figuration of the unfigurable. That is to say, of the imminence

of sense at its limit. Imminence of fullness in exhaustion, of tragedy in comedy—and vice versa. Of the too much in the too little. Imminence of the incommensurable.

Proximity heightens the incommensurable: a slight, infinitely diminutive but infinitely maintained distance, contact, touch, the point where representation blurs and the vertigo of presence begins. There where the simulacrum—the thin film of the other—ceases to simulate or rather never ceases to tumble into a simultaneous real. At once fucking and its fiction.

What fiction, then? Not so much the fiction of a narrative, of an adventure of seduction, fascination, or jouissance—because this precisely, the actuality of these phases, these scansions of the act withdraw from the ideality of words. I say "erotic novel" in order to suggest a history, the fact that sex takes place, that it is a-thing-taking-place—that outstrips itself, that opens beyond itself, that tells itself to itself, that recites itself as a role learned by heart, and that fictions itself, gives itself a figure, a fashion. That demands nothing, therefore, but to be said: to say what cannot be said but only done, and thus to do what cannot limit itself to being said, to saying-doing or doing-saying:

> Lady, i will touch you with my mind.
> Touch you and touch and touch
> until you give
> me suddenly a smile, shyly obscene
>
> (lady i will
> touch you with my mind.) Touch
> you, that is all,
>
> lightly and you utterly will become
> with infinite ease
>
> the poem which i do not write.[148]

This is why the only possibility of saying, here, arises there where sex and language happen to cross one another and for once to mix—to (dis)continue one another. There where, one might say, *logos*, *tekhnè*, and *eros* together become, for a time, the trinitarian condition of the self-relation of what is selfless (of what pulses). Speech that in saying acts—because no text is erotic through its "object" without being so through action as well. An art (technique) of doing that thereby convert itself into a supposed object (pornography). Desire of the desire to say its own act. An art that is supposedly practiced by those who listen (or read) as much as those who speak (or write).[149] Sex ex-pressing itself: one day, Simon Hantaï called one of his paintings *Sexpress* in "homage to Jean-Pierre Brisset"[150]—that is, to plays on words such as this one: "*Je sais que c'est bien. Je ou jeu sexe est bien.* The first *jeu* was sex." Hantaï adds: "a painting made one afternoon of erotic fascinations (the act of lovemaking united with the act of painting) with arbitrary orgiastic acts in a magico-erotic climate."[151]

*

What gives rise to the drive to say? Pasqual Quignard says that it is beauty. He writes:

> *Stendahl says from the first sentence of his prodigious book on love that fascination in action itself has a fascinating beauty.*
> *Then he says no more.*
> *But this is what drives him to write: love is beautiful.*[152]

How to bring about the crossing or the melee of sex and language—aside from silence or the cry into which they each plunge together or separately?

To remain within acceptable limits and not open an erotic anthology, I merely adduce six[153] cases or six brief examples (in addition to all the texts cited throughout this book):

The melee can consist in naming exactly, at the distance of words, the act in the process of happening as if it could be detached from I who name it and you who read it:

> I situated myself comfortably between his legs, in a position that allowed me to get at everything without moving. I could swallow his cock, suck his testicles, or stick my tongue in his sphincter. I felt like a baby bird feeding in his little nest.[154]

Another type of melee scrambles the tongue, speech, and/or writing with what it catches through passing contact, the heavy and elusive matter of the act:

> Last murmuring dregs of shell-like lips slipping off the Labrador coast, oozing eastward with the mud tides, easing starward in the iodine drift.[155]

One can (un)speak silence:

> (we die in silence, we
> enjoy shamefacedly—in silence, hiding
> our joy even from each other
>   keeping
> a secret joy in the flame which we dare
> not acknowledge)[156]

—or rather silence speech:

> How did Sappho and her women-friends talk among themselves? . . . They bring their bodies close and caress one another. Their conversation has freed itself from the subject and from language . . . Silence and

voluptuous delight—eternally divorced in conversa-
tion—have become one.[157]

A chiasmus of words can amount to sensate flesh:

SPASMS, I love you, psalms,
the feeling-walls deep in the you-ravine
rejoice, seedpainted one[158]

One can also say almost nothing about it and yet . . .

Is it too late to touch you, Dear?
We this moment knew—
Love Marine and Love terrene—
Love celestial too—
[. . .]
Betrothed to Righteousness might be
An Ecstasy discreet
But Nature relishes the Pinks
Which she was taught to eat—[159]

Unless, to conclude, one simply notates with a dash the
moment and place of the act—as Kleist does:

Here—he took, once she'd been joined by her terrified
ladies-in-waiting, the initiative, to call for a doc-
tor . . .[160]

Postlude

The drive propels and it threatens. Life blooms and exhausts. Desire arises, carries away and veers off or else goes extinct. Civilization blossoms and rips itself apart; it renounces obscenity and mobilizes violence. Sex is at the crossroads, where the turbulence of desire becomes love, where renunciation might renounce itself and open toward a higher art. Kant sees in sex a relationship between natural power and the art of receiving this power—masculine and feminine aligned with nature and culture. Freud does not think that love can appease destructive rage—but the parallel that he traces between sex and art upholds the drive's ability to find a form. That is, a way to make sense.

> *Pauli is hopping with desire. Elsa calms him down and they unite almost painlessly.*
> *"So, you like dates."*
> *Trying to catch their breath, their flushed heads come up from under the covers.*
> *Pauli kisses her, kisses her and closes his eyes.*

Elsa stares at him with her sea-colored eyes.

With a quick scream Pauli pulls out of Elsa. They stay interlocked for another long moment.

"What's that! Us, I mean," Pauli laments, "it messes me up."

"Have you ever . . . ?"

Pauli shakes his head. "You?"

"No. It hurts a little."

Pauli gets up. Staggers. "All your papers!"

Elsa holds a pillow tight against her chest and wraps her arms around her knees. "Pauli!" she murmurs.[161]

*

Superfluous Supplement

Still more? Not done yet?

It is not easy to escape the thrust of the drive once it finds an opening. The necessary wait for a book to appear in print sometimes tempts and sets traps for its author. Especially if the feeling already weighs on him not that he has more to say but, much to the contrary, that he is overwhelmed by what he wishes could be said and done far beyond what he knows himself capable of.

Two circumstances have arisen to exacerbate this feeling. The first: just recently, students in France were assigned a written exam on the topic of "the construction of the concept of the drive as the *Grundbegriff* of metapsychology." The second: Miquel Barceló, after reading the manuscript of this book made the painting that is now included in it.

What relationship is there between these two circumstances? The ground. It's a matter of the ground. *Grund-begriff*—a term that Freud employs several times in his text on the drives—signifies "fundamental concept" but could just as well be understood as a "concept of the ground." The drive is not only a fundamental concept for metapsychological thought: within this metaphysics stripped of "being" or "principle," it names the primordial thrust of existence or to existence. In this sense, it takes the place of the divine "prime mover." The sole distinction is that the latter is immobile whereas the drive is, by definition, mobility itself. From Aristotle to Freud the ground of all things is in motion. (One might add: passing through Hegel.) We know this even at the University (where one must be careful not to become sclerotic).

What Barceló paints here is less a ground or a source than points of access to the ground, ways of exposing oneself to it, straying into it, touching it. But above all, he paints right on the ground, right on the thickness of its supple substance, ever moving, sensitive, tender, agitated at the core of its turbid, earthly, and restless matter, which bears forms into its depths and opacity. He openly paints—it can be said—what no gaze can paint. He turns pornography inside out like a glove, a sweaty, silty, frothy glove. The hand that paints touches itself, daubed with its own gesture like the sexes daub each other with the thick fluids in which they seize one another, sink one another, and undo one another.

If Freud characterizes the drive as a "myth," it is because he grasps very precisely how the concept of the ground both posits and withdraws a ground that won't ever have the solidity of a foundation. As an archaeologist, he knows that, here, columns have no base and rest upon themselves—upon their own emotion. This insubstance is what sustains and ungrounds the ground of what "lives," what "feels" and "loves," "hates," "desires," "speaks" and, in silence, runs ever deeper. The myth is the self-expression of what nothing else can express or explain.

Painting is just the thing for not-saying — without thereby showing — this coloring, this running of the ground off on its way. It declares excess, exhibiting its superfluity. Yes, sex is superfluous and its overflowing of all necessity propels the astounding excess of sense that we unendingly undergo and enjoy.

Notes

1. Freely adapted from "Unaque res haec est, cuius quam plurima habemus / Tam magis ardescit dira cuppedine pectus" (Lucretius, *De natura rerum*, IV, 1089–90). "For love / Is unique: the more we have of it, the more it's not enough" (Lucretius, *The Nature of Things*, trans. A. E. Stallings [New York: Penguin Books, 2007]). "Love is unique; the more of it we have / The hotter our hearts burn with their fierce desire" (Lucretius, *On the Nature of Things*, trans. Anthony Esolen [Baltimore: Johns Hopkins University Press, 1995], 152). "Nothing else / Inflames us, once we have it, with desire / Of more and more and more" (Lucretius, *The Way Things Are*, trans. Rolfe Humphries [Bloomington: Indiana University Press, 1968], 151).

2. Michel de Montaigne, *Essays*, trans. M. A. Screech (New York: Penguin Books, 1993), 1262 [translation slightly modified].

3. Jacques Derrida, *Writing and Difference*, trans. Alan Bass (Chicago: University of Chicago Press, 1978), 186. (This passage is from a commentary on Artaud).

4. Lucretius, *On the Nature of Things*, trans. A. E. Stallings (New York: Penguin Books, 2007), Book IV, 1100–12.

5. Shoshana Felman writes: "[T]he human sexual act always

connotes the speech act — the act par excellence of the speaking
body, which subsists only insofar as it speaks, and which cannot
know whether it, or the fire that it carries, is after all really a
'thing' or only an 'event' . . . The sexual act, in the speaking
being, might be only a speech act" (Shoshana Felman, *The
Scandal of the Speaking Body: Don Juan with J. L. Austin, or
Seduction in Two Languages*, trans. Catherine Porter [Stanford:
Stanford University Press, 2003], 79).

6. Lucretius, *The Nature of Things*, VI: 1113–14.

7. Perhaps there is a pleasure in sharing itself: in friendship
(so important for Epicurus), in the festival, in the feast or the
banquet, in spectacle . . . But, in sex, the pleasure of sharing
(or communication) gives way to the sharing of pleasure, itself
perhaps unsharable. This motif, here, will form a basso continuo.

8. Lucretius, *The Nature of Things*, VI: 1114–19.

9. Michel Deguy, *L'Énergie de désespoir* (Paris: PUF/Collège
international de philosophie, 1998), 122.

10. On the basis of what Robert Muchembled calls "the erotic
mutation of the 18th century." Cf. *L'Orgasme et l'Occident* (Paris:
Seuil, 2005), 165.

11. To recall: the former was the author of the very famous
Psychopathia sexualis (1886); the latter is the title of a collection
of popular documents, stories, tales, and expressions of a sexual
nature published on a regular basis from 1859 until the beginning
of the twentieth century.

12. Joseph L. Mankiewicz, *The Late George Apley* (1947), film.
I take the occasion of this citation to note that literary or poetic
inclusions and intrusions will crop up throughout my discussion
as relays, allusions, or supplementary turns toward what discourse
alone doesn't suffice to speak or rather to announce. Everything
here hangs upon a desire to say what desire expresses or
experiences beyond words.

13. Sigmund Freud, "The Ego and the Id," in *The Standard
Edition of the Complete Psychological Works of Sigmund Freud*,
ed. and trans. James Strachey (London: Hogarth Press, 1961), Vol.
19, 44. (Hereafter SE.)

14. Ibid.

15. Ibid.

16. Not that long ago, within psychoanalysis itself, it was still necessary to recall that Freud's invention pertained most properly to Eros. See André Green, *The Chains of Eros: The Sexual in Psychoanalysis* (New York: Routledge, 2001).

17. Marcel Proust, *Swann's Way: In Search of Lost Time*, Vol. 1, trans. Lydia Davis (New York: Penguin, 2002), 161.

18. Priestess, possessor of divine knowledge, the figure of whom can be analyzed as a feminine double of Socrates who would thus be redoubled in two sexes, like Tiresias—himself the model for all soothsayers.

19. See the long note in Chapter VI of *Beyond the Pleasure Principle* (SEXVIII, 58). It is worth noting that the obscure joy thus obtained by the Hindu *Atman* is translated into German as *Freude*. Freud himself commented on this feminine version of his name. The necessary references can be found in Roger Dadoun, *Sigmund Freud* (Paris: L'Archipel, 2015).

20. In *The Erotic Phenomenon*, trans. Stephen E. Lewis (Chicago: University of Chicago Press, 2008), Jean-Luc Marion discussed this question. Without examining in detail his treatment of it, I note that he addresses the distancing by Heidegger (and then Lévinas) of the ontology that is affiliated with its disqualification: Eros remains foreign to "being" understood in terms of "beings," substance or *subjectum*. It is also in this sense that, in my own way, I would like to understand *existence*—that is, being-outside-self, as signaled in a primordial manner by the drive called "sex," a sexistence.

21. Plato, *Phaedrus*, trans. Alexander Nehamas and Paul Woodruff (Indianapolis: Hackett Publishing Co., 1995), 255c; 46.

22. Ibid., 250d, 39.

23. This is what Marie-Hélène Bohner-Cante does with striking verve in *Platonisme et sexualité* (Mauvezin: TER, 1981).

24. Immanuel Kant, *Critique of Pure Reason*, trans. Werner Pluhar (Indianapolis: Hackett Publishing Co., 1996), "Transcendental Dialectic," Chapter III, Section IV.

25. Throughout this history, Christian love obviously plays a considerable role. It would have to be studied in its own right.

For the moment, I limit myself to noting that it was very exactly in such love that a metamorphosis took place, over a very long period of time, of what, in philosophical Eros, was not invested in *phronesis*.

26. Meanwhile, this formula is only known to occur in two later authors, Haephestion and Eustathius of Thessalonica. The two words can be found associated in Euripides, in particular in verse 1135 of *Iphigenia at Aulis*. (Thanks to Claire Nancy and to Monique Trédé for these references.)

27. The context allows these terms to be translated as "constitution and circumstance" but it's not for nothing that Freud writes these words in Greek, which thus retain a mythical value in the sense that the drives are mythical: inseparable from the language that attempts to enunciate them.

28. We cannot not refer here to Rudolf Bernet, *Force, Drive, Desire: A Philosophy of Psychoanalysis*, trans. Sarah Allen (Evanston: Northwestern University Press, 2019).

29. Léopold Sédar Senghor, "Congo," trans. Melvin Dixon (Charlottesville and London: University Press of Virginia, 1991), 77.

30. Posthumus fragment in Karl Schlechta, ed., *Werke*, Vol. III (Munich: Carl Hauser Verlag, 1956), 909. (My translation, which retains *pulsion* for *Trieb*, since Nietzsche also uses the word *Instinkt*—J-LN.)

31. On these considerations as well as on "primary masochism," readers will find much of interest on pages 274–95 of Rudolf Bernet's book cited earlier, *Force-Drive-Desire*.

32. There exists one fertile study, by Cristian Ciocan, on the *Trieb* in Heidegger: http://www.ipjp.org/images/e-books/OPO%20Essay%2048%2020Sur%20le%20concept%20de%20pulsion%20(Trieb)%20chez%20Heidegger%20-%20By%20Cristian%20Ciocan.pdf.

33. We can also write, as Armand Zaloszyc does, "this real that ex-sists in relation to familiar everyday reality, which is impossible to bear" (*Freud et l'énigme de la jouissance* [Toulon: Éditions du Losange, 2009], 182). It is the same thing—the Thing that is never familiar.

34. [In English in the original.]

35. Friedrich Schelling, *Von der Weltseele* ("On the World-Soul") in *Werke*, Vol. 1 (Munich: Beck Verlag, 1927), 636. [The German text, which Nancy translated into French, and I have translated into English in consultation with his text, reads as follows: "Das Prinzip des Lebens ist nicht von außen in die organische Materie (etwa durch Infusion) gekommen—(eine geistlose, doch weitverbreitete Vorstellung)—, sondern umgekehrt, dieses Prinzip hat sich die organische Materie angebildet. So indem es in einzelnen Wesen sich individualisierte und hinwiederum diesen ihre Individualität gab, ist es zu einem aus der Organisation selbst unerklärbaren Prinzip geworden, dessen Einwirkung nur als ein immer reger Trieb dem individuellen Gefühl sich offenbart."]

36. Roberto Bolaño, *2666: A Novel*, trans. Natasha Wimmer (New York: Picador, 2009).

37. Jacques Lacan, *The Seminar of Jacques Lacan, Book XX: Encore, 1972–1973*, trans. Bruce Fink (New York: W.W. Norton & Co., 1998), 111.

38. Amaru, "Hundred Verses," in *Love Lyrics*, trans. Greg Bailey (New York: New York University Press, 2005), 273.

39. This word should be understood, in accordance with contemporary usage, in the generic rather than the gendered sense. This text is excerpted from Maurice-Merleau Ponty, *Phenomenology of Perception*, trans. Colin Smith (New York: Routledge, 1962), 183, 192–93.

40. In a footnote, the author specifies that this word is taken "in its etymological sense (without any Romantic overtone)."

41. D. H. Lawrence, *A Propos of* "Lady Chatterley's Lover" (New York: Haskell House, 1973), 11–12. From this point forward, I will invoke, in counterpoint to my discussion, different texts, mostly literary, as witnesses to what discourse does not suffice to say.

42. Joyce Carol Oates, *I Lock My Door Upon Myself* (New York: Ecco Press, 1990), 73.

43. [Translator's note.] A reference to the old French song, "La Rirette," otherwise known as "Jeanneton prend sa faucille" ("Little Jeanne takes her sickle." It tells the story of a girl who

meets "four handsome young boys" in the fields on her way to
cut flowers: the first caresses her chin; the second throws her on
the grass; the third raises her skirt . . . (the *soulèvement* to which
Nancy obliquely refers, implying that, in 1789, when the song
first appeared, this word would also have political overtones); and
then, the song declines to say what the fourth does, adding that,
to find out, you should go out into the fields yourself. The song's
complete lyrics are as follows: "Jeanneton prend sa faucille, / La
rirette, la rirette, / Jeanneton prend sa faucille, / pour aller couper
du jonc (bis) / En chemin elle rencontre, / La rirette, la rirette, / En
chemin elle rencontre, / Quatre jeunes et beaux garçons (bis) / Le
premier un peu timide, / La rirette, la rirette, / Le premier, un peu
timide, / Lui caressa le menton (bis) / Le deuxième un peu moins
sage, / La rirette, la rirette, / Le deuxième un peu moins sage, / La
jeta sur le gazon (bis) / Le troisième encore moins sage, / La
rirette, la rirette, / Le troisième encore moins sage, / Lui souleva
son blanc jupon (bis) / Ce que fit le quatrième, / La rirette, la
rirette, / Ce que fit le quatrième, / N'est pas dit dans cette chanson
(bis) / Mais pour le savoir Mesdames / La rirette, la rirette, / Mais
pour le savoir Mesdames / Allez donc couper du jonc (bis) / La
morale de cette histoire, / La rirette, la rirette, / La morale de
cette histoire, / C'est qu'les hommes sont des cochons (bis) / La
morale de cette morale, / La rirette, la rirette, / La morale de cette
morale, / C'est qu'les femmes aiment les cochons (bis).")

44. This is another way of approaching the Lacanian maxim,
of which I offered a commentary in my previous book, *L'il y a
du rapport sexuel* (Paris: Galilée, 2001). An English translation
(*The "There Is" of the Sexual Relation*) can be found in *Corpus II:
Writings on Sexuality*, trans. Anne O'Byrne (New York: Fordham
University Press, 2013), 1–22.

45. Paul Verlaine, "Ars Poetica," in *One Hundred and One
Poems by Paul Verlaine: A Bilingual Edition*, trans. Norman R.
Shapiro (Chicago: University of Chicago Press, 1999).

46. Arthur Rimbaud, *Rimbaud: Complete Works, Selected
Letters*, trans. and intro. Wallace Fowlie (Chicago: University of
Chicago Press, 2005), 73.

47. Entirely independent of one another, Arash Aminian

Tabrizi and I have resorted over the past few years to the forms
"s'exister" and "sexistence." He was the one who noticed it and
let me know. He will publish something about this. In addition,
Mehdi Belhaj Kacem has spoken of "*sexêtre*" [sex-being] in
order to designate an ontological sexual difference (see *Être et
sexuation* [Paris: Stock, 2013]. In the present discussion, without
opposing Belhaj Kacem as such, sexual difference will only come
into question after the examination of a sexicity—nondifferential
or rather always in the process of differentiation, pregnant with
multiple differences.

48. "*On s'est trouvés / Rien n'est perdu / Nous sommes éperdus /
On va le prouver*" [We found each other / Nothing was lost / We
are lost in love / We will prove it], Jacques Dutronc et Françoise
Hardy.

49. As soon as infinity is in question, one confronts—in
language and in the real—the daunting entanglement of what
Hegel calls "bad infinity" (number, the interminable) and "good
infinity," unnameable in the strict sense (although set theory
made it possible to calculate) or "true" as in Spinoza, for whom
"substance" (being) is infinite as absolute—that is, unbound
from everything, identical to its own solitary presence and
manifestation. The knotting, sharing, and ambiguity between the
two is constantly at play, in a remarkable fashion, within language
and in sex, each seeking to absolutize itself and/or interminably
to start anew. This entanglement must be kept in mind each time
the question of infinity arises.

50. This suggestion comes from Heidegger although he also
somehow let it drop . . . Writing *Sein* in the archaic fashion
as *Seyn* has no impact on the substantive—and he forgets that
"being" is entirely confused with "ex-." Here is not the place to
take up this discussion.

51. Elsewhere, it would be necessary to examine the
provenance of Christian desire itself, between the Greek *eros* and
Biblical sex, as well as the Muslim developments of desire.

52. Why a therapy? Because the drive suffers, as I have said,
and thus it makes suffer. More exactly, it *is* suffering and pleasure
intermixed: being as pushing itself pursues, perseveres, as well as

refuses this effort, slips away. Existing bears itself forth *and* cannot bear itself. It is possible that this intimate contradiction, today, is reaching its height, and that the illness of civilization produces at once the idea of care and the vivid consciousness of its inanity (the consciousness that Freud articulates in *Civilization and Its Discontents*). This suffering, we believe, is just as treatable as any other, by lifting or diverting repression. But it's an entire civilization that suffers, for which there is no care. It suffers not from repression but rather from the extreme pressure of its own libidinal infinity. It's not out of the question, however, that this infinity might be grasped or invested otherwise. All other civilizations have known how to treat the forcing that gave rise to them: for instance, among many others, the Buddhist or Taoist teachings on suffering.

53. Serguëi Essenine [Sergei Yesenin], *Cette nuit*, https://www.espritsnomades.net/litterature/serguei-essenine-linsurge-de-la-poesie-le-frere-du-vent/?mots-cles=essenine# [translated from the French].

54. Israel Joshua Singer, *The Brothers Ashkenazi*, trans. Joseph Singer (New York: Other Press, 2010), 318.

55. Victor Hugo, *Les Miserables*, trans. Norman Denny (New York: Penguin, 1982), 763.

56. Here I would refer to the work of Juan-Manuel Garrido, *On Time, Being, and Hunger: Challenging the Traditional Way of Life* (New York: Fordham University Press, 2012).

57. Alberto Moravia, *The Conformist*, trans. Angus Davidson (New York: Farrar, Straus and Young, 1951), 261. This reflection on "nature" might be prolonged through that of Emanuele Coccia in *The Life of Plants*, trans. Dylan J. Montanari (New York: Polity Books, 2018), especially Chapter 13, entitled "Reason is Sex."

58. Baruch Spinoza, *Ethics*, V, 42. In *Complete Words*, ed. Michael L. Morgan, trans. Samuel Shirley (Indianapolis: Hackett, 2002), 382 [translation slightly modified].

59. Pascal Quignard, *Critique du jugement* (Paris: Galilée, 2015), 96.

60. The word "erotism," for Bataille, designates human sexual

activity as it becomes independent of an exclusively reproductive function. In what I'm sketching here, this possibility is augured by the homology, which I discussed above, between sex and language. I prefer not to use a term that, since Bataille, has gone from sulfurous to smelling like a rose. On the other hand, it is not certain that there is no animal erotism. Finery, dances, odors, and mating calls, are they simply lures into the act of reproduction? It has often been considered that, in human beings, desire is such a lure, a ruse of nature. This does not make much sense. Why would a lure be necessary in the first place? We will come back to this.

61. Georges Bataille, *Erotism: Death and Sensuality*, trans. Mary Dalwood (San Francisco: City Lights, 1986), 11.

62. Ibid., 13.

63. Ibid., 15.

64. [In English in the original. — Trans.]

65. Audre Lorde, "The Uses of the Erotic: The Erotic as Power," in *Sister Outsider: Essays and Speeches* (Berkeley: Crossing Press, 2007), 59.

66. Jacques Derrida, *Dissemination*, trans. Barbara Johnson (Chicago: University of Chicago Press, 1981), 53.

67. Joë Bousquet, *Le Cahier noir* (Paris: Albin Michel, 1989), 177 (thanks to Romana Recchia Luciani).

68. Arthur Rimbaud, *Rimbaud: Complete Works, Selected Letters*, trans. Wallace Fowlie, updated and revised, and with a foreword by Seth Widden (Chicago: University of Chicago Press, 2005), 169.

69. Lacan gives "fantasy" a very particular sense and role that I leave aside here because I do not situate myself within his perspective.

70. Schelling utilized the word "anorgic."

71. Literally, "stories of ass." Roughly akin, in English, to the way in which "skin" functions as a metonymy for sex in the expression "skin flicks." In English, in a somewhat different manner, "ass" can also function as a figure for sex in general (as in expressions such as "to get some ass").

72. Michel de Montaigne, "On Some Lines of Virgil," in

The Complete Essays, trans. M. A. Screech (New York: Penguin, 1991), 1992.

73. Edith Wharton, "Beatrice Palmato: A Fragment," in Gloria C. Erlich, *The Sexual Education of Edith Wharton* (Berkeley: University of California Press, 1992), 176.

74. Gustave Flaubert, "To Mlle. Levoyer de Chantepie. Croisset, February 8, 1859," in *Correspondance*, Vol. III (Paris: Gallimard, 1991), 16–17 (thanks to Jean-Pierre Daumard).

75. What Freud calls the "unconscious" is not "nonknowledge": much rather, it is the play libidinal forces. If the nature of these forces is a "myth" their combined action is not one.

76. Hélène Cixous, *Le rire de la Méduse* (Paris: Galilée, 2010), 78.

77. Truman Capote, *Answered Prayers* (New York: Knopf, 2012), 101.

78. Paul Celan, "Spasms," in *Breathturn into* Timestead: *The Collected Later Poetry, A Bilingual Edition*, trans. Pierre Joris (New York: Farrar, Strauss, & Giroux, 2014), 121.

79. Claude Simon, *The Flanders Road*, trans. Richard Howard (New York: Georges Braziller, 1961), 261–62.

80. G. W. F. Hegel, *Phenomenology of Spirit*, trans. Terry Pinkard (Cambridge, U.K.: Cambridge University Press, 2018), 181.

81. He evokes pleasure briefly later in the text in a discussion of the sexual organ in analogy to the hand as a tool turned toward an external object and that lacks the "self-reflection" found in the other manifestation that is physiognomy, in which he is forced to take an interest because of the "physiognomy" of his time, and that he critiques because the interior cannot be adequate to external contingency. This is precisely what I move away from here, opposing irreducible difference to any claim to adequation. Accordingly, it must be said that the hand and the sexual organs are not simply devoid of "self-reflection"; and it must be considered that sexual physiognomy (the mimicry of desire and enjoyment) merit special attention.

82. In Derrida's *Glas* can be found an analysis of Hegelian sexuality.

83. Without dwelling on the point, I will add this: that

existence has three dimensions implies that it does not have one unique sense—which can also be understood to mean: no sense at all. In fact, each of these dimensions ceaselessly transcends or slips away, whichever one prefers; elsewhere, we shall ask whether this trinity has anything to do with Augustine's (intellect, memory, will) or that which he borrows from Hilaire (eternity, beauty, usage): each time—as in the divine trinity—at stake is the triple self-relation of what does not subsist in itself.

84. G. W. F. Hegel, *Phenomenology of Spirit*, 181.

85. Philippe Sollers, *Paradis II* (Paris: Gallimard, 1986), 98.

86. On the subject of transformation, see the works of Boyan Manchev, for which the first necessary indications can be found in *Rue Descartes*, No. 64 (2009).

87. Gilles Deleuze, "Description of a Woman: For a Philosophy of the Sexed Other," trans. Keith W. Faulkner, *Angelaki*, Vol. 7, no. 3 (December 2002), 21–22.

88. Michel Surya, *L'Impasse* (Marseille: Al Dante, 2010), 37.

89. There is no dearth of scholarly or "curious" collections of tales, legends, stories, expressions, songs, and images of a sexual nature.

90. Pierre Jean Jouve, *Les Beaux Masques*, in *Œuvre*, Vol. II (Paris: Le Mercure de France, 1987), 1630. (Thanks to Gisèle Berkman.)

91. The same thing could be said if one sought to shake the kaleidoscope of ritual, customary, or cultural practices of all human and animal groups; all the observances, all the markings, the prohibitions, the sources of shame and pride, the words, the gestures, the outfits, and the spiritualities that from prehistoric times have swirled around sex.

92. Jacques Derrida, *The Post Card: From Socrates to Freud and Beyond*, trans. Alan Bass (Chicago: University of Chicago Press, 1987), 145, cited and studied by Rosaria Caldarone in Juan Manuel Garrido, Rosaria Caldarone, and Jean-Luc Nancy, "La tulipe, l'androgyne et le vulgaire: Sexe in Derrida," *Rue Descartes*, Nos. 89–90 (2016), 158–71.

93. Sigmund Freud, *Three Essays on the Theory of Sexuality*, trans. James Strachey (New York: Basic Books, 1962), 84.

94. Sigmund Freud, *The Ego and the Id*, SEXIX, 38. It could be added that, because the German *Ich* is at least as much "I" as "Me," in the speaking being the Me also distinguishes itself precisely as a speaker and that it is thus necessary to understand how there is a sexual calling-itself-I as well as a self-distinguishing-itself.

95. Matthew 5:28.

96. Vivant Denon, *No Tomorrow*, trans. Lydia Davis (New York: NYRB Classics, 2009), 25.

97. James Joyce, *Brouillons d'un baiser* (Paris: Gallimard, 2014). Marie Darrieussecq's remarkable translation into French is accompanied by Joyce's original text.

98. Georges Bataille, variant of *L'être indifferencié n'est rien*, in *Œuvres completes*, Vol. III (Paris: Gallimard, 1971), 560.

99. Watch, too, John Cameron Mitchell's *Shortbus* (2006). With a quite beautiful vigor, this film traverses—in order to salvage it—the unruliness of polymorphous sex.

100. Cf. Georges Didi-Huberman's study of figure in *Fra Angelico: Dissemblance and Figuration*, trans. Jane Marie Todd (Chicago: University of Chicago Press, 1995).

101. Thanks to Peter Banki and John Paul Ricco.

102. Walt Whitman, "A Woman Waits for Me," in *Leaves of Grass and Other Writings* (New York: W.W. Norton & Co., 2002), 87.

103. [In English in the original. —Trans.]

104. Meg Bogin, *The Female Troubadours* (New York: Paddington Press, 1976), 89.

105. Shakespeare, Sonnet VIII.

106. Pier Paolo Pasolini, *C.*, trans. Isabella Checcaglini and Étienne Dobenesque (Paris: Ypsilon, 2008). [Translated from this French translation.]

107. Walt Whitman, "Dalliance of the Eagles," in *Leaves of Grass and Other Writings*, 229.

108. Charles Baudelaire, "To a Woman Passing By," in *Flowers of Evil*, trans. James N. McGowan (Oxford: Oxford University Press, 2008), 189.

109. Alenka Zupančič, *L'éthique du réel. Kant avec Lacan* (Paris: Nous éditions, 2009), 95. [These lines do not appear in the English edition of this book, which differs significantly from the French edition.] Cited in Bernard Baas, "Ulysse en Baltique," *Filozofski vestnik*, Vol. 35, no. 2 (2014), 11–32. This text offers a particularly remarkable discussion of *jouissance*.

110. Jean Racine, *Phaedra*, in *Iphigenia, Phaedra,* and *Athaliah*, trans. John Cairncross (New York: Penguin, 2004), 161.

111. Louise Labé, *Love Sonnets & Elegies*, trans. Richard Sieburth (New York: New York Review Books, 2014), 26.

112. Marcel Proust, *In the Shadow of Young Girls in Flower: In Search of Lost Time*, Vol. 2, trans. K. Scott Moncrieff, ed. William C. Carter (New Haven: Yale University Press, 2015), 112 [translation slightly modified].

113. Abdelwahab Meddeb, *Talismano*, trans. Jane Kuntz (New York: Dalkey Archive Press, 2011), 184–85.

114. The philosopher in question is Michel Henry. See *L'Essence de la manifestation* (Paris: Presses Universitaires de France, 1963), 860, and the entire section that leads up to this page. But a comparable situation can be found in many other thinkers. For example, this citation from Mallarmé that Derrida adopts for his own purposes: "Pyrotechnical no less than metaphysical, this point of view; but a sort of fireworks, at the height and on the example of thought, makes ideal enjoyment light up with bloom" (*Dissemination*, 54). Likewise, Merleau-Ponty gives a privileged place to Eros: "Erotic perception is not a *cogitatio* which aims at a *cogitatum*; through one body it aims at another body, and takes place in the world, not in a consciousness" (*Phenomenology of Perception*, 181).

115. Walter Benjamin, "Goethe's *Elective Affinities*," in *Selected Writings, Volume 1: 1913–1926*, ed. Marcus Bullock and Michael W. Jennings (Cambridge: Harvard University Press, 2004), 335.

116. On this topic, see Rudolf Bernet's forceful analyses of Husserl within the double horizon of Heidegger and Lacan in the above cited work, *Force—Drive—Desire*.

117. Louis-Ferdinand Céline, *Journey to the End of the Night* (New York: New Directions, 2006), 408.

118. Tiresias—who alternated between man and woman, who as a soothsayer traversed generations, who himself lived for seven generations and whose death constituted the very source of his life. He is the one who, in addition, made Oedipus confront the truth of his destiny. One of his most recent literary descendants is the sex-changing character Carlo in Pasolini's novel, *Petrolio*. Carlo changes his sex twice; he becomes a woman and then becomes a man again; and he thereby shows himself as the truth of division and succession reunited: "All of human history, or so it seems, does nothing but repeat one thing: there *is* only what *has been*. And in fact, Carlo, undressing, saw that *what had already happened to him was happening to him* . . . in the mirror . . . he saw Polyhymnos again, rather than Polyhymnia, or, if you like, Baubo rather than Baubon" (Pier Paolo Pasolini, *Petrolio*, trans. Ann Goldstein [New York: Pantheon, 1997], 433).

119. As written in the *Encore* seminar, from which here, in this very book, it gives pleasure to recall the text: "a jouissance of the body, that is, if I may express myself thus—why not make a book title out of it? It'll be the next book out from Galilée—beyond the phallus. That would be cute, huh?" I don't have the audacity to pretend that the present book is cute enough for Lacan's cohort, but does not set out to displease them . . . [The passage from *Encore* that Nancy cites in this passage refers to *The Title of the Letter*, co-written with Philippe Lacoue-Labarthe and published by Éditions Galilée in 1973.—Trans.]

120. Michèle Gennart, *Corporéité et présence* (Argenteuil: Le Cerle herméneutique, 2011), 209.

121. Benoît Goetz, "Un sexe à la Leiris," in *Le Portique* 36 (2016), 1–5.

122. E. E. Cummings, *Complete Poems, 1904–1962*, ed. George J. Firmage (New York: Liveright, 1991), 218.

123. Antonio Moresco, *Gli Incendiati* (Milan: Mondadori, 2010), 33. (Thank you, Cécile.)

124. Pierre Jean Jouve, *Les Beaux Masques*, in *Œuvre II*, 1614.

125. This is an aspect that Lacan very judiciously highlights in the same text.

126. Friedrich Schlegel, *Erottische Soneten*, Sonnet 4, http://www.zeno.org/Literatur/M/Schlegel,+Friedrich/Gedichte /Erotische+Sonette. [The English translation is mine, in consultation with Nancy's French version.] It is notable that the subject of this sonnet sequence engages alternately in hetero- and homosexuality, pedophilia, and auto-eroticism.

127. Alfred de Musset to Georges Sand, September 1, 1834.

128. Georges Bataille, *The Poetry of Georges Bataille*, trans. Stuart Kendall (Albany: SUNY Press, 2018), 53.

129. Jean-Luc Godard's film, *Weekend* (1967)—made a few years before the two significant films that I discussed above—is devoted, as we know, to a kind of polymorphous massacre by means of car accidents, sordid murders, and revolutionary executions; but it also features a sort of prelude, which is the story a woman tells her companion about a round of group sex in which she participated without him. The story finished, the man says that she got him excited—and then the film cuts to the first images of cars. Later will come a parodic scene of ritualized sex, in which an egg and then a fish are substituted for the penis (thank you Mathilde Girard).

130. Conrad Aiken, "This Dance of Life," *Turns and Movies, and Other Tales in Verse* (Boston: Houghton Mifflin, 1916), 86–87.

131. This observation is primed by Leo Strauss, who undertakes, from his specific perspective, a detailed analysis of the end of the *Symposium*. See *On Plato's "Symposium"* (Chicago: University of Chicago Press, 2003).

132. Jacques Derrida, "Psychoanalysis Searches the State of Its Soul," in *Without Alibi*, ed. and trans. Peggy Kamuf (Stanford: Stanford University Press, 2002), 280.

133. Ingeborg Bachmann, *Darkness Spoken: The Collected Poems*, trans. Peter Filkins (Brookline: Zephyr Press, 2006), 455.

134. Pier Paolo Pasolini, *Petrolio*, trans. Ann Goldstein (New York; Pantheon, 1997), 278–79.

135. Cf. Spinoza, *Ethics*, Part V, Proposition 4, *Scholium*, in *Complete Works*, trans. Samuel Shirley (Indianapolis: Hackett, 2002), 365. I owe the basis for this analysis to François Zourabichvili, *Spinoza, une physique de la pensée* (Paris: Presses Universitaires de France, 2002), 216. And this analysis should be compared to Bernard Pautrat's study, *Ethica sexualis: Spinoza et l'amour* (Paris: Payot, 2011)—which Zourabichvili would have done himself if he had been alive to do it. I do not claim to replace him. But it seems to me that my approach to "cannot be excessive" makes it possible to bring them together.

136. Paul Audi, *Le pas gangné de l'amour* (Paris: Galilée, 2016), 176.

137. There is a film that shows, rather happily, the necessity of hiding what must be hidden: *Une liason pornographique* (Frédéric Fonteyne, 1999).

138. Jean-François Lyotard, *Les Transformateurs Duchamp / Duchamp's TRANS/formers* (Leuven: Leuven University Press, 2011), 193. Lyotard immediately comments that Duchamp seemed to favor the second hypothesis. [Translation slightly modified.—Trans.]

139. For the moment, I leave aside any anatomical and physiological considerations of the organs predisposed or supposed to produce pleasure—all of the erectile organs (clitoris, penis, vagina, nipples) over which sexanalysts like to linger—because each of them only "functions" inside a set that overflows organicity and function. Every zone can become erotogenic: this also means that *eros* gives birth to a different body, a pulsive or impulsive body. No less desirable, undoubtedly, are the new *blasons of the body* (as they used to say) wherein are symbolized cocks, lips, fingers, glands and glans, cavernous bodies, hairs, mucous membranes, and vestibules.

140. Georges Bataille, *La Scissiparité*, in *Œuvres complètes*, Vol. III (Paris: Gallimard, 1970), 228.

141. Robert Alexis, *Nora* (Paris: José Corti, 2010), 109.

142. Olivier Rolin, *Veracruz* (Lagrasse: Verdier, 2016), 113.

143. Michel Deguy, *Gisants* (Paris: Gallimard, 1985): "I drank at your nadir / leading you it could be to be more" (66).

144. "Many people wish to speak of the thing. Because they know that it has a unique quality. It foments an intensity without intimacy" (Philippe Beck, Sexicité, 2003, https://www.sitaudis.fr /Incitations/sexicite.php).

145. Cf. Her interview about *Destroy, She Said*; https://m.ina .fr/video/I05125289/marguerite-duras-a-propos-de-detruire-dit-elle -video.html (thanks to Mathilde Girard). In the same interview, she adds that prostitutes have confided to her that they often receive the declaration, "I love you."

146. Jean Paulhan, "Happiness in Slavery," Introduction to Pauline Réage, *The Story of O* (New York: Ballantine Books, 2013), xxxii.

147. Georges Bataille, *Erotism: Death and Sensuality*, trans. Mary Dalwood (San Francisco: City Lights Books, 1986), 276.

148. E. E. Cummings, *Complete Poems: 1904–1962*, 983.

149. Catherine Millet remarks that there is a certain vocabulary that "if it is used carelessly . . . acts on the senses almost as directly as physical contact" (Catherine Millet, *The Sexual Life of Catherine M.*, trans. Adriana Hunter [New York: Grove Press, 2003], 215). Dante says, for his part, when he thinks he sees the fusion of all things, "for, speaking this, I feel / A joy that is more ample" (*Paradiso*, trans. Allen Mandelbaum [New York: Everyman's Library, 1995]. XXXIII, 93).

150. September 18, 1955. Collection of the Centre Georges Pompidou. See also, Jean Pierre Brisset, *La grammaire logique, suivi de La Science de Dieu* (Paris: Tchou, 1970).

151. Archives of the Centre Georges Pompidou, AM 1976–972.

152. Pascal Quignard, *Vie secrete* (Paris: Gallimard, 1998), 461 (thanks to Isabelle Howald). To be more precise, I will add that Quignard continues: "Love is more beautiful than concupiscence." But the point is not to "spiritualize" love because he also speaks of the "sap that haunts bodies," the bodies of lovers.

153. From the Latin homophone *sex*.

154. Alexander Garcia-Düttmann, "Paul Does Not Bake Cakes," in *Gegen die Selbsterhaltung* (Berlin: August Verlag, 2016), 125. [Translated from Nancy's French translation.]

155. Henry Miller, *Tropic of Capricorn* (New York: Grove Press, 1994), 108.

156. William Carlos Williams, *Paterson* (New York: New Directions, 1995), 117.

157. Walter Benjamin, "The Metaphysics of Youth," in *Selected Writings, Volume 1: 1913–1926*, ed. Marcus Bullock and Michael W. Jennings (Cambridge: Harvard University Press, 1996), 10.

158. Paul Celan, *Breathturn Into Timestead: The Collected Later Poetry*, 120.

159. Emily Dickinson, *The Complete Poems of Emily Dickinson*, ed. Thomas H. Johnson (Boston: Little, Brown & Co., 1960), 672.

160. Heinrich von Kleist, "The Marquise of O," in *Selected Prose of Heinrich von Kleist*, trans. Peter Wortsman (Brooklyn: Archipelago Books, 2010), 96 [translation slightly modified]. The German text reads: "Hier—traf er, da bald darauf ihre erschrockenen Frauen erscheinen, Anstalten, einen Arzt zu rufen . . ." [Nancy cites this sentence fragment in his own translation, about which he comments: "my translation freely opens up the sentence in order to convey what is more palpable in the German: the verb that follows the dash suggests that this mark dissimulates a different action verb, or perhaps the same one: 'he takes—the woman who fainted.' In addition, the German *Hier* can be rendered by 'here' in the sense of 'at this point in the story'; for, we know the whole story that ensues from this act. Thank you, Hélène."]

161. Hanns Zischler, *La Fille aux papiers d'agrumes*, trans. J. Torrent (Paris: Christian Bourgeois, 2016), 90–91. [My translation is from the French translation of the German.]

Jean-Luc Nancy is Distinguished Professor of Philosophy at the Université Marc Bloch, Strasbourg. His wide-ranging thought is developed in many books, including *Portrait, The Possibility of a World, The Banality of Heidegger, The Disavowed Community*, and *Corpus*.

Steven Miller is Associate Professor of English and Director of the Center for Psychoanalysis and Culture at the University at Buffalo, SUNY. He is the author of *War After Death: On Violence and Its Limits* and the translator of books by Catherine Malabou, Étienne Balibar, and Anne Dufourmantelle.

Printed and bound by CPI Group (UK) Ltd, Croydon, CR0 4YY

09/06/2025

14685656-0001